THE CORRIS RAILWAY

THE STORY OF A MID-WALES SLATE RAILWAY

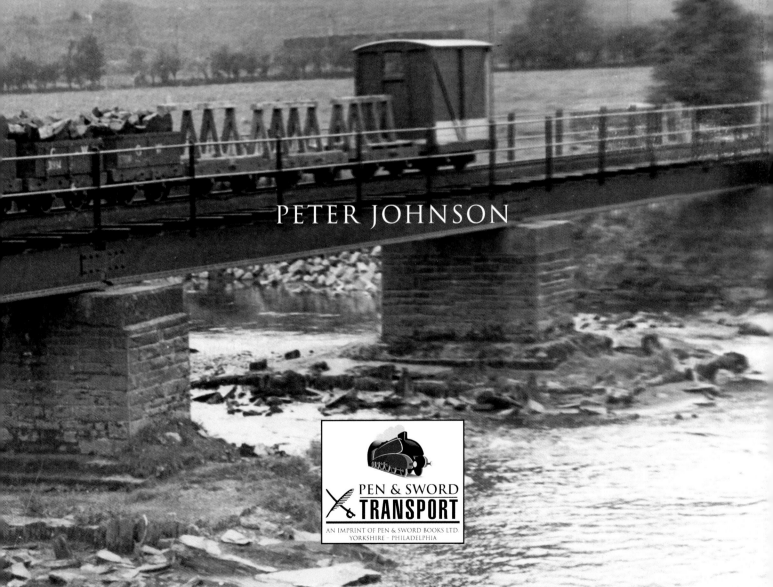

THE CORRIS RAILWAY

THE STORY OF A MID-WALES SLATE RAILWAY

PETER JOHNSON

PEN & SWORD
TRANSPORT

AN IMPRINT OF PEN & SWORD BOOKS LTD.
YORKSHIRE - PHILADELPHIA

FRONT COVER: No 2 with a passenger train at Machynlleth in 1899.

REAR COVER:
UPPER: No 3 and its train at Corris shortly before the railway closed. (John Norris/John Scott Morgan collection)

LOWER: No 4, the only locomotive bought by the Corris Railway Company, approaches Corris on 24 October 1996.

ENDPAPERS: The Corris Railway's route highlighted on the 1902 edition of the 6in Ordnance Survey. (Crown Copyright reserved)

TITLE PAGE: The Corris Railway's location, mostly in a narrow valley, makes the taking of photographs of trains in the landscape almost impossible. The one accessible location where the scenery opened up was the Dyfi River Bridge, as seen with this view of the 'Tattoo' crossing the river with three wagons of coal for the village and three empty slab wagons for Aberllefenni in the 1930s. (John Scott Morgan collection)

First published in Great Britain in 2019 by
Pen and Sword Transport

An imprint of Pen & Sword Books Limited
Yorkshire - Philadelphia
Copyright © Peter Johnson, 2019

ISBN: 978 1 52671 753 5

Typeset by Aura Technology and Software Services, India
Printed and bound in China through Printworks Global Ltd.

Pen & Sword Books Limited incorporates the imprints of Atlas, Archaeology, Aviation, Discovery,
Family History, Fiction, History, Maritime, Military, Military Classics, Politics, Select, Transport, True Crime,
Air World, Frontline Publishing, Leo Cooper, Remember When, Seaforth Publishing,
The Praetorian Press, Wharncliffe Local History, Wharncliffe Transport,
Wharncliffe True Crime and White Owl.

For a complete list of Pen & Sword titles please contact

PEN & SWORD BOOKS LIMITED
47 Church Street, Barnsley, South Yorkshire, S70 2AS, England
E-mail: enquiries@pen-and-sword.co.uk
Website: www.pen-and-sword.co.uk

Or
PEN AND SWORD BOOKS
1950 Lawrence Rd, Havertown, PA 19083, USA
E-mail: Uspen-and-sword@casematepublishers.com
Website: www.penandswordbooks.com

CONTENTS

ACKNOWLEDGEMENTS AND SOURCES

This book is founded on the Corris Railway history contained in *An Illustrated History of the Great Western Narrow Gauge* (Oxford Publishing Co, 2011), which is out of print, and thus incorporates material extracted from the records of the Corris Railway Company, Aberystwyth & Welsh Coast Railway, Great Western Railway, British Railways, the Court of Chancery and the Board of Trade housed at the National Archives, Kew, Parliamentary records held in the House of Lords and Imperial Tramways' reports made available to me by Richard Greenhough. To this corpus has been added material extracted from digitised newspapers held in the British Newspaper Archive (www.britishnewspaperarchive.co.uk) and the National Library of Wales' Welsh Newspapers Online collection (www.newspapers.library.wales). Use has also been made of the Corris Railway Society's annual reports, reports published in *Railway Magazine* and my own contributions to *Steam Railway* magazine since 1995. Bringing these sources together has enabled a more detailed history of the railway, its origins and its revival to be constructed than any previously published.

Only a small number of photographs of the Corris Railway were taken before the 1920s and previously unpublished ones are rarely found, which accounts for the use here of images with which some readers may be familiar. From the 1920s, enthusiasts were regular visitors and new collections occasionally surface to be added to the small pool of photographs that exist of this period and enabling the use of some unpublished images here. The railway's restricted loading gauge and the nature of the terrain through which it passed, and passes, also limits the choice of locations available to photographers, resulting in some similarity in images.

The task of illustrating the book would have been made more difficult were it not for the efforts of Donald George, a Scotsman who trained in photography with the famous Dundee postcard publisher James Valentine. Marrying a Welsh woman in 1888, he settled in Upper Corris and photographed the area extensively, publishing numerous postcards of his photographs until his death in 1944. Eleven of them are used here.

Michael Bishop, Robert Darlaston, Tim Edmonds, Martin Fuller, Mike Green, John Scott Morgan, Mark Stephenson and Dave Waldren supplied photographs from their collections and I extend my grateful thanks to them. Uncredited photographs are either from my collection or of my taking.

Martin Fuller and Ed Castellan kindly commented on the text.

A few illustrations that are technically deficient have been selected for their historical merit. I am responsible for any errors.

Peter Johnson
Leicester
July 2019

WELSH PLACE NAMES

Many Welsh places frequented by outsiders accrued Anglicised versions of their names. Being in a relatively remote location, this did not occur in the Dulas valley, misspellings of Aberllefenni appearing to be more in error than intention. Elsewhere, Aberystwyth was sometimes rendered Aberystwith in the nineteenth century and Aberdyfi as Aberdovey, Dolgellau as Dolgelley and Tywyn as Towyn until the 1970s.

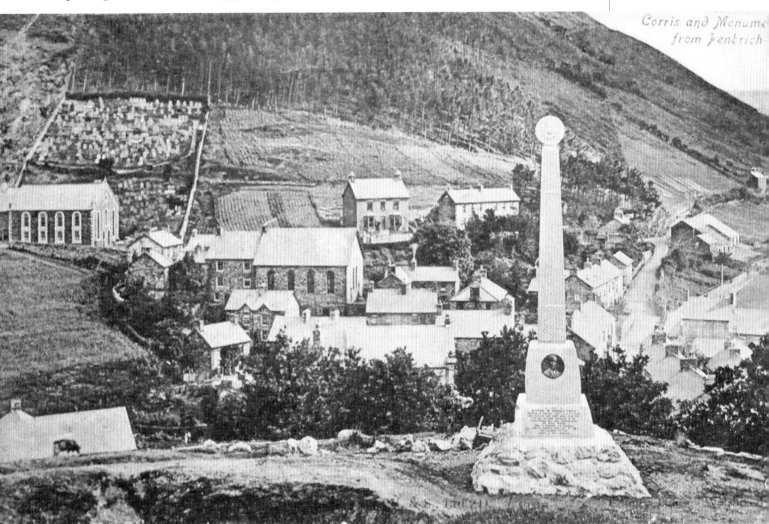

Corris and Monume... from Penbrich

A view of Corris in the early 20th Century. The village's two chapels, and its cemetery, are visible and the Corris Railway's route to Aberllefenni can be seen on the right of the picture. The memorial to Alfred William Hughes was erected by public subscription. Born in the village in 1861, he became Professor of Anatomy at Kings College, London, but died of fever during the Boer War in 1900. (J. Valentine)

INTRODUCTION

Located in the Dulas valley, just to the north of Machynlleth, a market town on the banks of the Dyfi some ten miles from the Cardigan Bay coast at Aberdyfi, the 2ft 3in gauge Corris Railway had to overcome obstacles not faced by other railways.

The directors were in dispute before it was built, it was expressly forbidden to use steam locomotives, the quarry owners objected to its carrying passengers and then, after approval had been obtained for the use of steam locomotives and the carriage of passengers, the Board of Trade refused its sanction because it had not been built in accordance with the deposited plans.

Notwithstanding these difficulties, it was still the second public narrow gauge railway in Wales, following the Festiniog Railway further north. With its restricted loading gauge responsible for its tiny locomotives and its quirky tramcar carriages, the railway became an essential feature of life in the valley.

When passenger services were eventually introduced, the railway's management took advantage of its location on one of the main routes to the tourist haunts of Cader Idris and Talyllyn by running road services thence, connecting with the train service. The widespread advent of motor transport after the First World War led to charabancs replacing horse-drawn carriages and an expansion of road services.

From 1878, ownership by the Imperial Tramways Company protected the railway from the commercial realities of the outside world, the owner underwriting its losses. Sale to the Great Western Railway when Imperial was liquidated in 1930 transferred the railway to another benevolent owner, albeit one who reduced its operations to a minimum by withdrawing passenger services soon after taking control.

Nevertheless, the railway was to continue until nationalisation in 1948, when the threat of the Dyfi bridge embankment being breached by flooding led to its closure later in the year.

Unlike the Talyllyn Railway, operated by volunteers from 1951, the Festiniog Railway, reopened from 1955, and the Welshpool & Llanfair Light Railway, reopened from 1963, there was no rush to revive the Corris Railway. Indeed, when enthusiasts first looked at it, their only thought was to develop a museum.

However, their vision was soon expanded to include an operating railway in their plans and a society was formed. Battling not only against the issues that arise from the railway's remote location and its unusual track gauge, a small group has fought against bureaucratic intransigence and changing rules to bring their plans to fruition, culminating in the start of passenger services on a short section of track in 2003, the first phase of several intended to restore trains to the Dulas valley. It is a fascinating railway, and worthy of the efforts being made to revive it.

The Corris Railway Company's seal, as applied to legal documents.

CHAPTER 1

THE HORSE ERA

The slate quarries of Corris and Aberllefenni were located five and six miles to the north of Machynlleth, an ancient market town in the old county of Montgomeryshire, now part of Powys. The town sits just above the flood plains on the southern banks of the Afon Dyfi, River Dovey in English, ten miles from the Cardigan Bay coast. The Romans settled in the locality, a fort known as Maglona was built on the ridge on the river's northern bank, and a market charter was granted in 1291. By 1851 the population was 1,665. The river was navigable by smaller craft to within two miles of the town, and deep water was available on the coast at Aberdyfi. In 2009 the Dyfi valley became the first UNESCO Biosphere in Wales, fulfilling conservation, development and logistical functions.

The quarries were set in the Dulas valley, the west bank of the river in Merionethshire and the east in Montgomeryshire, enclosed by mountains rising to more than 1,500ft, the main centre at Corris. At around the 100ft contour there is little level ground in the locality to be dogmatic about its precise elevation.

First recorded in the fourteenth century, investment in local slate quarries in the 1830s brought growth to the village too. By 1861 the population was 1,565 but 150 years later it had fallen to 723, which reflects both the loss of employment opportunities and the desire of the inhabitants to have more personal space.

To the north-west of Corris lies the Deri valley, where the Braich Goch quarry tips once dominated the village and where the smaller Gaewern and Abercorris quarries were located. To the north-east, further along the Dulas, were the Aberllefenni and Ratgoed quarries. There were other

quarries too, but these were the most significant. As a quarrying centre, the Corris area was much smaller than Ffestiniog, Dinorwic, Nantlle or Penrhyn to the north. The slate was not as fine as that produced at the Ffestiniog, Dinorwic and Penrhyn centres, but was suitable for slabs and enamelling.

During the 1830s, newspaper advertisements give a flavour of the economic development of some of the quarries: purchasers or partners wanted, Gaewern, next to Braich Goch, (*North Wales Chronicle* 21 June 1831); North Wales Slate & Slab Company, £80,000 capital required to develop Rhognant (Ty'n y Berth), and Tyn y Ceunant, next to Gaewern (*Worcester Journal* 4 August 1836); Braich Goch, to let (*North Wales Chronicle* 19 June 1838); British Slate & Slab Company, £15,000 capital to develop Abercorris, opposite Gaewern (*Hereford Journal* 11 July 1838).

Abercorris was on the east side of the Merionethshire turnpike from Dolgellau, the county town, the others on its west side, just to the north-west of the village. Crossing to the eastern side of the Deri, the turnpike shared the Dulas valley with the river as far as its union with the Dyfi at Fridd Gate. The road had been improved in the 1830s, the 1838 advertisement for the Braich Goch quarry lease describing it as 'new', giving it an even gradient favouring the transportation of slate to the Dyfi.

From Fridd Gate it was the practice to take the slate across the Dyfi to wharves on the southern bank at Derwenlas and Morben. There it was transhipped to small craft capable of navigating the river to the harbour at Aberdyfi where it was transhipped again to coastal trading craft. The Dyfi was first bridged in 1533, the current structure dating from 1805 being listed grade II*.

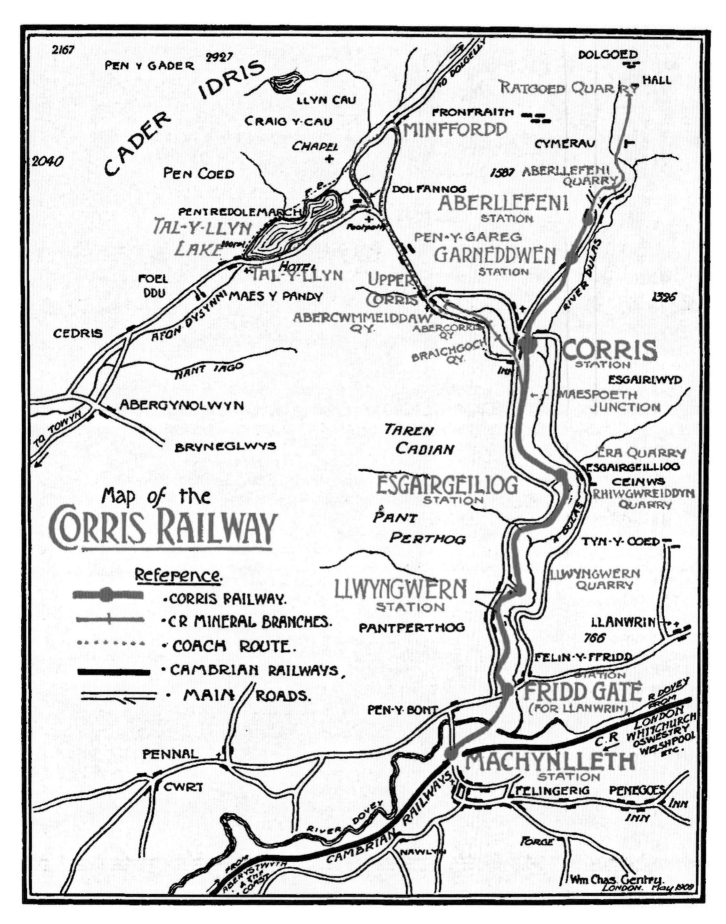

Produced in 1909, this graphic showing the railway and its surroundings was used on timetables and in issues of the company's reports to shareholders.

DOVEY BRIDGE, MACHYNLLETH. 20083.

The Dyfi river bridge near Machynlleth. The route of the railway crosses the centre of the picture in a straight line, the railway's river bridge almost obscured by trees. The Cambrian Railways' line to Newtown runs along the bottom of the hills on the far side of the river. (Donald George)

Although there is nothing to show for them now, the Derwenlas wharves were well established. As well as slate, lead from the Dylife mines, between Llanidloes and Machynlleth, was also exported and ships were built there in the early nineteenth century, the last being a 160-ton schooner named *Sarah Davies* launched in April 1870. Ships had also been built at Morben, the last being a 400-ton brig launched in 1865.

The motivation for the railway did not, directly, have its origins in the locality, but in Gloucester. At some time in the 1840s, a group of investors from that place had taken over the Braich Goch quarries and had started to develop them. When the Braich Goch Slate & Slab Quarry Company was floated in 1851, the managers were named as Thomas Wakeman Esq of Chalfont St. Giles, Buckinghamshire, and Robert Jackman Esq, Arthur Causton Esq, civil engineer, William Rees Esq, architect, and William Wingate Esq, builder, all of Gloucester. Running the quarry was their agent, Thomas Smith Nicholls, another Gloucester man.

Perhaps looking northwards, and noticing how the Ffestiniog, Dinorwic and Bethesda slate quarries had benefitted from increased output and profitability

since they had started transporting their production by rail, in 1850 the Braich Goch owners decided that they should have a railway too.

The first public manifestation of their decision came with a public meeting held at the Machynlleth town hall on 7 August, reported in the *Carnarvon & Denbigh Herald* under the heading 'Abercorris and Aberdovey Railway'. The meeting, not as well attended as it might have been because it coincided with a fair, resolved that a railway between those places 'would be attended by many advantages, both to the landed and trading interest of the neighbourhood, and the quarry proprietors …' There was no mention of any public interest. Tribute was paid to Causton, who had prepared the plans and sections for the proposed line.

Born in Gloucester in 1811, the youngest son of a printer, and newly elected, in May 1850, Gloucester city surveyor, Causton's nomination for election as an associate member of the Institution of Civil Engineers in 1846 had stated that he had more than ten years' experience as a surveyor working on his own account, 'chiefly engaged recently

Braich Goch quarry's slate stacking yard and sheds. The railway's Tyddynyberth branch ran between the road and the quarry buildings and then through the bridge behind the dressing sheds. The bridge carried a track used to carry waste from the underground quarry to the spoil tips. (County Times, Welshpool)

with Mr [James Meadows] Rendel and Mr [Isambard Kingdom] Brunel'.

His engagements with these notable engineers may be slightly overstated as they seem to relate only to work carried out during a brief period in 1844. In October Rendel had appointed him to make surveys for the Gloucester & Dean Forest Railway, which might have been the extent of his participation in that undertaking, and in December he had made tidal observations in connection with the Great Western Railway's proposal to bridge the Severn at Newnham, Gloucestershire, receiving a good soaking when he narrowly escaped being washed away by the bore.

The intention to deposit a Bill for the Corris, Machynlleth and River Dovey Railway or Tramroad was advertised first in the *Carnarvon & Denbigh Herald* on 16 November. The road between promoting a Bill and building a railway, however, was to be long and tortuous.

The Bill called for the powers to construct and operate a 'line from the Aberllefenny slate quarries to the River Dovey, with branches'. The notice described it as 'a railway or tramroad

commencing at or near the engine house at Aberllefenny slate quarries … and terminating at or near a certain house called or known as Panteidal, on the river Dovey …', near the western end of the later Aberystwyth & Welsh Coast Railway's Aberdovey tunnel No 1, together with branches 'from and out of the line of the intended railway or tramroad hereinafter described, commencing at or near a house called or place known as Aberllefenny … and terminating … at or near a certain house called or known as Tycam. Also, a branch railway or tramroad … commencing in the township of Corris … at or near the fifth milestone on the turnpike road leading from the town of Machynlleth to the town of Dolgelley … and terminating at or near a certain house called or known as Tyddynyberth.'

Measured from Aberllefenni, the deposited plans showed a 13-mile main line with a viaduct 572 yards long taking it over the Afon Pennal, near Talgarth Hall, and a tunnel 68 yards long on a two-chain curve near Llugwy Hall, both on the northern bank of the Dyfi. The branches were shown with lengths of

An extract from the Corris, Machynlleth & River Dovey Tramroad's deposited plan, 1850. (Parliamentary Archives)

THE FIVE POINTS, THE ESTUARY, ABERDOVEY.   W.340.

1 mile 6 furlongs 2 chains to Tycam and 2 miles 1 furlong to Tyddynyberth. The ruling grade to the former was 1 in 38 and 1 in 35 rising to 1 in 25 for the latter. On the estuarial section, the gradient averaged 1 in 660 whereas on the valley section it was 1 in 113 to the location now known as Maespoeth and 1 in 112 to Aberllefenni. The sharpest curves were of two chains, three along the river, one on the Tyddynyberth branch and two on the Tycam branch. As coastal craft were expected to be able to sail up to it, the terminus at Panteidal would eliminate transhipment to river craft, reducing costs and breakages.

In contrast to the route adopted when the railway was eventually built, from the Dyfi bridge as far as Maespoeth the route followed an alignment on the western side of the road. The branches were more tram-like in their alignments and mostly followed the road exactly. The mixed nature of the alignments must be responsible for the 'railway or tramroad' uncertainty over the scheme's title. Finding routes that avoided existing structures, particularly around Corris, must have

taxed Causton, who signed the £12,000 estimate.

In the newspaper, the notice was followed by a prospectus for the Corris, Machynlleth & River Dovey Tramway Company dated 9 September 1850, which sought to raise £12,000 in £1 shares. Declaring that the quarry proprietors had guaranteed an output of 6,500 tons a year, which, at 3d per ton, would yield up to £960 15s, and forecasting a further £625 income by abstracting two-thirds of the 12,365 tons (merchandise, coal, limestone) landed at Aberdyfi each year, and calculating working expenses (four men, three horses, wagon repairs, clerk and office) at £400, the promotors predicted an ample profit. Landowners had given their approval to 11¾ miles of the 16 miles. Setting the rate of call at 2s 6d was intended to encourage small investors.

Due to unspecified disagreements between the promoters, named as Captain Thruston RN, Robert Davies Jones, Francis Johnson Ford, John William Rowlands, Captain Groves HETCS, and David Davies, all local men, the Bill was withdrawn

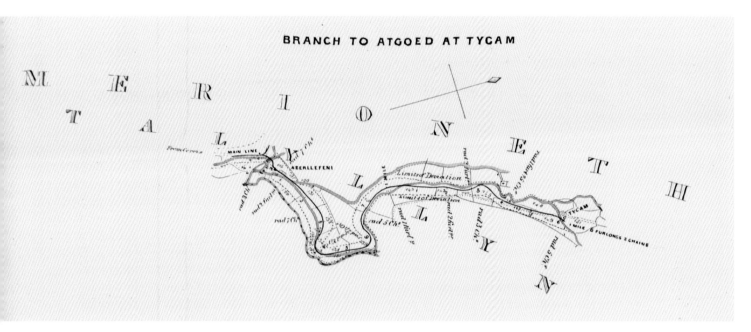

Detail of the deposited plans for the branch to Tycam, otherwise known as the Ratgoed Tramway. (Parliamentary Archives)

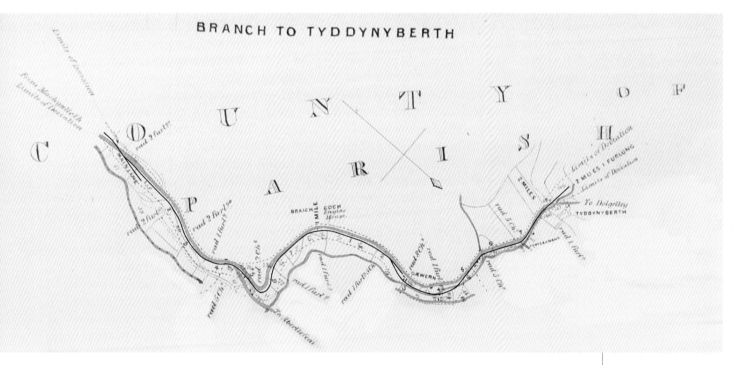

Detail of the deposited plans showing the junction at Maespoeth, the main line to Gaewern and the branch to Tyddynyberth.

before any Parliamentary consideration could be given to it.

A year later, it was resubmitted. On this occasion the services of Henry Brookes, a Parliamentary agent, were used in preference to a Machynlleth solicitor. Several landowners objected, mounting a campaign that resulted in three of the promoters withdrawing. On 23 March 1852 the Lords committee resolved to dispense with the standing orders and allow the Bill to proceed providing the promotors proceeded within three days. They obviously did, because the Bill was enacted as the Corris, Machynlleth & River Dovey Railway Act on 1 July 1852, the last day of the Parliamentary session. Notwithstanding what the prospectus had said, the first call for shares was 10s per share, although the first advertisement, on 3 April, had called for £10, a corrected advertisement being published without comment the following week.

The Act identified the promoters as the Viscount Seaham, R.D. Jones, John Rowlands, F.J. Ford, J.W. Rowlands and David Davies, and designated them as the first directors. Despite the title, the Act still contained numerous references to tramroads and the company was to be incorporated as the 'Corris, Machynlleth & River Dovey Railway or Tramroad Company'. Constraints were placed on the limits of deviation where the line was to pass through property belonging to Seaham, the late Athelstan Corbet, Charles Thomas Thruston and Mary Matthews.

The nature of the railway, its purpose and method of working were described quite succinctly in article No 24 – 'The said railways or tramroads, being intended for the conveyance of slates, minerals, and merchandise, and to be worked by horse-power travelling at low rates of speed only, it shall be lawful to construct the same upon a gauge of 2ft 2½in; provided always, that it shall not be lawful to use or employ any steam or locomotive engine on the railways or tramroads …' On any occasion that a locomotive was used in contravention of the act a penalty not exceeding £20 was payable. Three years were allowed to exercise the compulsory purchase powers and five years for construction.

Brookes, the Parliamentary agent, was to say that the promoters' desire to use the narrow gauge resulted in the company's inability to use locomotives being imposed by the House of Lords' committee, also that it had been intended to carry passengers as well as merchandise but an exemption from the 1846 Gauge Act was not obtained. As much of the route was in the parish of Talyllyn,

adoption of a different naming convention could have seen the enterprise called the Talyllyn Railway.

A week after the Act had received the royal assent, the Shrewsbury & Aberystwyth Railway Company issued its prospectus and it became obvious that the narrow-gauge line could attract 'pleasure and mercantile traffic' from Birmingham and the Midlands if it made a branch across the Dovey to join the proposed standard gauge line at Machynlleth, extended its line to Towyn and could carry passengers.

Brookes claimed that he had suggested promoting the ideas with a public meeting in Machynlleth but disagreements again occurred and nothing was done. Concluding that the directors were refusing to act to bring the company into effect and conscious that the company's first ordinary meeting had to be held by 30 September, he considered himself its *de facto* secretary and representative of the company's solicitor, who was absent, and decided to act, on 13 September, calling a meeting to be held on the last possible date.

Perhaps stirred on by Brookes' activities, the directors met for the first time on 29 September 1852, but J.W. Rowlands and Jones disagreed over the strategy for dealing with the deposit so the meeting was adjourned.

At Brookes's meeting the next day, Seaham, Jones and Davies were re-elected directors and James Smith, Charles Brown Hornor, William Fenton and Edward Stanway were elected. Brookes was appointed secretary with authority to prepare share certificates and other documents. It was resolved to seek powers to amend the act, to extend the line to Machynlleth and Towyn and to raise further capital, and to commission the engineer to report on the feasibility of extending the line to Carnarvon.

A notice advertising the intention of depositing a Bill for the Corris, Machynlleth, Aberdovey & Towyn Railway was placed in the *London Gazette* published on 23 November 1852. Two days after publication the original directors applied

for an injunction to prevent Brookes from acting on the company's behalf, including 'soliciting any Bill in Parliament', in their petition referring to the 'pretended meeting' and saying that three of the new directors were either not shareholders or held insufficient shares to qualify as a director and had repudiated their appointments.

As now proposed, the railway from Aberllefenni to Towyn would have been about twenty miles long, with the branch to the Aberystwyth line at Machynlleth slightly more than half a mile long. It was to run from 'a farm house, called or known as Penrhyn, at a field numbered 64 on the plans of the Corris, Machynlleth & River Dovey Tramroad … using the route of the said tramroad westward … to a point called Panteidal … and continuing … past Aberdovey and terminating at the southern side of a road diverging westward from the village of Towyn to the seashore … Also a branch railway, commencing … at or near a farm there, called or known as Penrhyn, at a field numbered 64 on the aforesaid plans, and proceeding southward from the above point, crossing the river Dovey and the turnpike road from Machynlleth to the Dovey bridge, and forming a

junction with the proposed Shrewsbury & Aberystwyth Railway in a field northward of the Machynlleth National School house and eastward of the turnpike road from Machynlleth to the Dovey bridge … Also a branch railway … commencing at or near a point upon the river Dovey shore, about a quarter of a mile east of a point of a rock at Aberdovey, called Penhelig Point, and continuing westward along the river shore on to a dock wall proposed to be erected to enclose Penhelig Bay …'

Causton had resurveyed the estuarine section, easing the curvature in several places at the expense of lengthening the tunnel to 158 yards and providing a second, 198 yards long. With 14 arches, spans up to 30ft wide and up to 20ft high, the viaduct, had it been built, would have been one of the most imposing structures on any British narrow-gauge railway. Facing Aberdyfi, the branch to the Shrewsbury & Aberystwyth Railway required a viaduct 402 yards long to cross the Dovey. The railway also intended to take powers to create an enclosed dock at Penhelig. The SAR's bill was deposited at the same time; both were withdrawn before the Parliamentary process could be started.

Detail from the Corris, Machynlleth, Aberdovey & Towyn Railway's 1852 plan, showing the branch crossing the river to join with the proposed Shrewsbury & Aberystwyth Railway. (Parliamentary Archives)

The approaching deadline for the use of the compulsory purchase powers spurred John Carnau Morris, Robert Davies Jones, John Rowlands and David Davies, quarry owners, into action in May 1855. Deciding to act as directors, they decided that the railway should be terminated at Pumwern, on the Dovey's northern bank, opposite Derwenlas, and served notices to treat on the affected landowners, which triggered a legal response from Earl Vane, formerly Viscount Seaham, who owned the land occupied by the Braich Goch quarry.

Acting with his wife, on 25 July he sought an injunction against the company, claiming that it was acting illegally, alleging that shortly after the passing of the 1852 Act the undertaking was abandoned or considered to be abandoned, that the directors, including Vane, had never been re-elected, that no calls had been made to shareholders and that the deposited monies had been 'misapplied or otherwise disposed of'.

Without the terminus at Panteidal, they continued, the railway would be useless for the purpose of transporting goods to and from Machynlleth, land transport being more convenient, claiming that the alleged directors intended to make the railway for their own benefit, not for the benefit of the company or the public. They sought a declaration that the company had no power to make a shorter railway and that the actions carried out in the company's name were illegal and an injunction preventing the railway from being made to Pumwern only, to stop construction and for the land to be returned.

After several exchanges and a court hearing the company, with support from the under-sheriff of Merioneth, took possession of the land on 30 June 1855, the day before the 1852 Act's compulsory purchase powers expired.

Having taken possession, it took the threat of another deadline, that for the work to start within five years, before there was any action on the ground, although the only reported comment about it was published in *Baner ac Amseru Cymru*, a Welsh-language newspaper, on 29 July 1857. The lack of any attempt to stop work must be taken as an indication that it was legally compliant with the deadline. The paper noted that construction had started at Aberllefenni quarry and commented that the area was run down, anticipating that the railway would revive the economy.

In November 1857, therefore, notices for another Bill were published, to give legal effect to the directors' intention not to build the railway to Pant Eidel. The only problem to arise during the Parliamentary process was that the Bill had been technically in breach of standing orders because the notice had not been published in any London newspapers, a requirement for any Bills involving land in more than one county, but when the omission was shown to be 'through inadvertence' it had been allowed to proceed.

Consequently, the second Corris, Machynlleth & River Dovey Tramroad Act received the royal assent on 12 July 1858. Of the 1852 Act, the Lords committee had inserted a reference to it in the preamble, saying that no part of the railway had 'yet been completed' and that the powers had lapsed.

The new Act's description of the main line, a tramroad, from Corris to the Dyfi, was much the same as before, starting 'at or near the slate quarry yard and new engine house at Aberllefenny slate quarries' but this time the line crossed the river and terminated 'at or near an old pier or landing place called … Cae Coch or Red Quay, at Garreg, on the river Dovey', otherwise near Glan Dyfi Castle, about three-quarters of a mile beyond the later Dovey Junction station, 11¾ miles in all.

Three branch tramroads were also permitted. Firstly, a short line from the Morben lower wharf to the south bank of the Dyfi at Penforddnewydd, the new road; secondly, a line commencing 'at or near the fifth milepost on the turnpike road … and terminating at or near the engine house at

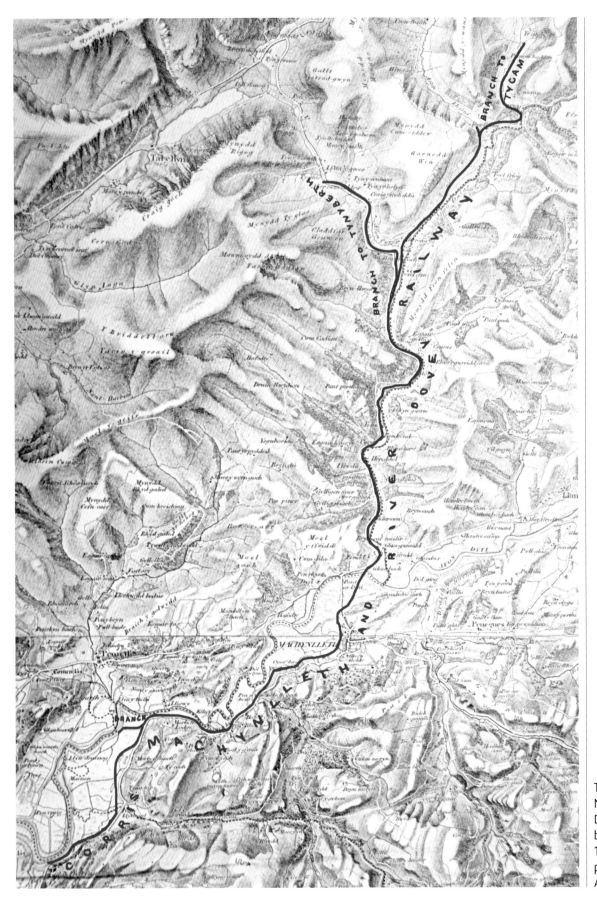

The Corris, Machynlleth & River Dovey Railway and branches, from its 1857 deposited plan. (Parliamentary Archives)

An extract from the Corris, Machynlleth & River Dovey Railway plan showing the Garreg route with the Aberystwyth & Welsh Coast Railway route overlaid. Realigning the river to accommodate the standard gauge route also had the effect of disconnecting the river from the Derwenlas wharves and in recent years the site has been filled in. (Parliamentary Archives)

Tyn y berth [previously Tyddynyberth]', and thirdly, 'commencing at or near the new engine house at Aberllefenny, and terminating at or near a certain house called or known as Ty cam [Tycam]'.

The plans show that the greatest change from the previous proposals was between Maespoeth and the railway's Dyfi bridge, where it had been moved to the east side of the road for nearly four miles, most likely to avoid Earl Vane's land. The minimum radius was five chains, which also applied to the section south of the river. Here the route was a mixture of roadside and cross-country. At 2 miles 5 chains, the Tyddynyberth branch was slightly shorter than before and the route at Caewern had been realigned to avoid a double river crossing. The Tycam branch was unchanged.

Concerning the nature of the railway, the House of Lords committee had inserted, at article No 20, article No 24 from the 1852 Act, which referred to the gauge and the use of locomotives, increasing the gauge to 2ft 3in and the penalty for the use of locomotives to 'not exceeding' £100 on each occasion.

Apart from its later adoption by the Campbeltown & Machrihanish Railway in the Mull of Kintyre, in Britain the use of the 2ft 3in gauge for public railways was to be restricted to an area with a radius of less than ten miles from Corris, its origin here probably attributable to its use on tramroads within the quarries. The nearby Mawddwy Railway, which was standard gauge, was allowed to be not less than 2ft 3in gauge in its 1865 Act of incorporation too.

The promoters on this occasion were Thomas Frederick Halford, Frank

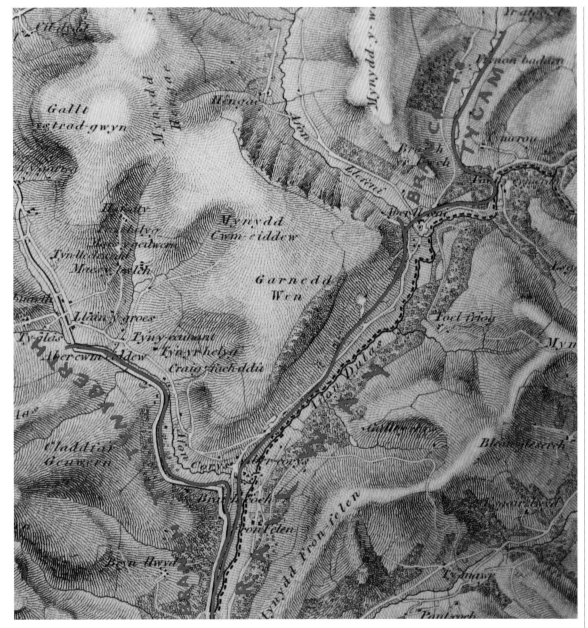

Howard, Horatio Nelson Hughes, John Rowlands and John William Rowlands, also nominated the first directors; only the last two remained from the 1852 scheme. Hughes was a Liverpool merchant and ship owner who also owned the Ratgoed quarry. Permitted to incorporate the Corris, Machynlleth and River Dovey Tramroad Company, they could only take any land required by agreement. Four years were allowed to complete the works, which Causton now estimated to cost £15,000, the amount of the authorised capital.

Armed with fresh powers, work was continued and sufficiently advanced by 18 September 1858 for the *Hereford Times* to carry an advertisement seeking 'one or two platelayers, for a tramway, in North Wales', applications to T.S. Nicholls, the Braich Goch agent, at Corris.

On 12 January 1859, the *Oswestry Advertiser* reported that the tramway from Abercorris to Machynlleth was 'fast approaching completion' and on 29 January the *North Wales Chronicle* reported that heavy rain and floods in the Dyfi had tested the stability of the new tramway's

One of the earliest representations of the Corris Railway, this lithograph of Machynlleth shows two horses hauling eight wagons towards the Dyfi bridge. An agglomeration of buildings is to be seen on the station site and the Aberystwyth & Welsh Coast Railway station behind that.

river bridge. The advertisement must have had the desired result, for the line opened between Corris and Machynlleth on 1 April 1859.

An account in the *North Wales Chronicle* of 9 April reported that 'Friday afternoon was celebrated as a holiday in the … neighbourhood' … 'the full working of this line, on its final completion to the coast, will insure to the public a saving in carriage, of about 50% upon the present system of conveyance by wagons and carts.'

In November 1878, incidentally, an *Aberystwyth Observer* contributor said that he had been told that T.S. Nicholls had been responsible for the idea of a railway, surveying a route in 1850. As the same contributor also claimed that the first 'tram' had crossed the Dyfi on 30 April 1859, a month after the public had gathered to watch 'the first transit of goods by railway to Machynlleth' (*North Wales Chronicle*

9 April), the claim for Nicholls should be treated with caution; he is not mentioned in any contemporary documents seen by the author. In 1859/60, he was advertising enamelled slate goods from the Corris slate works and in 1876 he was described as a land surveyor. He died in Corris in 1879.

Work to complete the line on the south of the river was apparently not rushed, for on 16 July the *North Wales Chronicle* reported that the 'second portion … is being made with energy and determination which will ensure its entire completion before next winter sets in', acknowledging Causton's 'diligence and perseverance' in carrying out the work. After the railway was completed he moved to Liverpool, where in 1862 financial difficulties led to him assigning his Merioneth property to his creditors. Later, trading as a surveyor and auctioneer in Walthamstow, Essex, he was adjudged bankrupt in 1871. Discharged in 1878, he moved to Hackney and died in

The Corris Railway formation on the made-up ledge below the parallel road near Pantperthog.

St Leonard's, Sussex, with an estate valued at £750, on 21 July 1885.

The tramroad had been built cheaply, to reduce the land needed. Between Fridd Gate and Corris it closely followed the road, without too much regard, it transpired, to the exactitudes of the deposited plans. Where there was insufficient space for the formation, sawn slate was used to build an embankment wall parallel to the road, the void probably being filled with slate waste. The newspaper's optimism that the 'second portion' would be completed before the winter was probably fulfilled as there were no further reports. The Aberystwyth & Welsh Coast Railway's 1861 10 inch to the mile plan indicates that it terminated a short distance from the river just to the west of Derwenlas, but this may be an error. The plan also contradicts claims made elsewhere that the railway was omitted from AWCR plans for nefarious reasons.

The Tyddynyberth branch would be referred to as the Braich Goch branch after the largest quarry that it served.

To enthusiasts, it became known as the Upper Corris tramway. The Tycam branch was always known as the Ratgoed tramway.

There is no contemporary report of the tramroad as built although a lithograph shows two horses hauling a train of nine wagons, possibly of three different types, downhill on the Tyddynyberth branch. There are reports that, like the Festiniog Railway contemporaneously, the loaded traffic was worked by gravity with horses based at Machynlleth returning the empty wagons to the quarries.

In 1872 the railway reported that it possessed 'only a few slate trucks', a statement that probably wouldn't have been inaccurate in 1859. Edouard Vignes (see bibliography), who visited Wales in 1877, was unable to elicit any details of its construction. Archaeology has revealed that the track was laid with lightweight bridge-section rail on slate sleepers; examples of the rail and a single sleeper are displayed in the museum at Corris.

This fine slate retaining wall is near Llwyngwern.

The railway formation to the right of the road looking towards Corris, on the edge of Aberllefenni. These walls were probably constructed when the formation was improved for the introduction of passenger services in 1887.

Running across the fields, between two lines of slate fences, the formation towards Aberllefenni on the edge of Corris remains clear to the interested traveller.

Another early railway view, this one showing a train on the Upper Corris branch. It has passed the Braich Goch Hotel and approaches Maespoeth, passing a stage coach on the road. How often, if at all, horses pulled wagons downhill is not known. From this perspective the route towards Aberllefenni should have been visible but the artist has not drawn it in beyond the trees.

Corris viewed from across the valley after 1900, with the 1878 station to the left of the tree in the foreground and the Braich Goch quarry workings behind. (Donald George)

At Abercorris, Abercwmeiddau quarry tips (left) face the Gaewern tips on the opposite side of the road. Both quarries were served by the railway. Cader Idris stands on the skyline. (John Thomas/National Library of Wales)

Corris, Upper Corris and Cader. 36476.

Extremities of the Upper Corris branch at Abercorris. The line to the right served Abercwmeiddau quarry, its incline cutting through the slate tips, which are now largely obscured by trees. The branch to the left merely served the village. Both branches survive as footpaths. The quarry closed in 1905. (Donald George)

Seen from opposite the Braich Goch Hotel, the Vale of Aberllefenni stretches off into the distance, the boundary of the railway route between Maespoeth and Corris visible on the far side of the field. (Donald George)

VALE OF ABERLLEFENNI. 20348.

HENGAE VALLEY AND CADER IDRIS. ABERLLEFENI. 18190.

The Aberllefenni slate quarry conducted work on three sites, quarrying on either side of the Hengae valley and dressing in the sheds on the lower left. (Donald George)

An unusual feature of this Aberllefenni incline, on the left of the photograph above, was its use of two gauges. The broad gauge track, carrying newly-quarried slate bound for the dressing sheds, was counter-balanced by wagons loaded with slab on the narrow gauge track, which would then be used to haul the empty broad-gauge trolley back up to the adit. It was derelict when seen in October 1978. (Dave Waldren)

The northern side of the Aberllefenni workings seen in July 1965. (Michael Bishop)

This 1925 view of Aberllefenni's dressing shed not only features wagons loaded with slate slab, but a single-bladed point and a pair of chickens scratching in the dust.

This July 1963 view of the dressing shed not only gives a better idea of its setting but also some minor changes that had taken place over the intervening years. In this case though there are no chickens scratching in the dust but a small child. (Michael Bishop)

The Dyfi bridge must have been poorly built, because on 28 August 1875 the *Aberystwyth Observer* reported that it was being renewed. Coincidentally, the old one had collapsed under the weight of four 'trams' loaded with building stone on 21 August, which had been intended to be its last day in use before it was replaced.

When first opened, the tramroad attracted little attention, although it was held responsible for the death of F.J. Ford, a local landowner and one of the original directors, on 14 August 1861. Driving home in his dog cart at 10.30pm on a dark, moonless night after an evening in Machynlleth, he took the Llwyngwern turn off the turnpike and one of the cart's wheels hit the track and turned it over, throwing him out with fatal results.

At the inquest, 'The jury consider it their duty to censure the tramroad directors for their great negligence for leaving the road so long in so dangerous and unprotected a state and not placing proper protections

Ratgoed was rarely visited by enthusiasts. Here a crane was used to haul stone out of the pit. October 1978. (Dave Waldren)

One of the first directors of the Corris, Machynlleth & River Dovey Railway or Tramway, Francis Johnson Ford, was killed when his dog cart turned over on the level crossing at Llwyngwern on 14 August 1861. He is buried with his wife and one of his sons in the churchyard of St Peter's, Machynlleth.

The nature of the fencing erected after F.J. Ford's death in 1861 is unknown. This fencing, near Llwyngwern, was probably erected when the line was adapted for steam traction in 1878.

The Braich Goch Inn, showing the Upper Corris branch level crossing in the foreground. If the uneven road surface is indicative of all the railway's crossings then the problem experienced by F.J. Ford can be more easily understood. (Donald George)

against accidents, which neglect in this case has occasioned the loss of a most valuable life in this neighbourhood. The jury wish also to draw the attention of the directors to other parts of the tramroad which they consider equally dangerous, and which ought to be fenced without delay.'

The jury seems to have overstepped the mark in this case, for no evidence was called about the tramroad or the state of the crossing, and fencing the tramroad would not have prevented an accident at an ungated crossing. Some fencing was put in hand, for on 9 April 1864 the *North Wales Chronicle* reported the prosecution of one Richard Jones (alias Dick Pwll Llan), charged with breaking fence wire belonging to the company with the intention of stealing it. The manager was in court but 'did not press the charge very much', hoping that it would be a warning. Jones was fined 5s, costs and damages.

By December 1862 the proprietors had deposited a Bill for fresh powers, including an extension, but its progress through the legislature was not straightforward. Headlined as an extension from Tycam to Tir Stent and Dolgelly, the notice describes a route from Tyddynyberth to a junction with the then proposed Bala & Dolgelly Railway near Brithdir, about three miles from Dolgelly.

Instead of just describing the extension, the notice described the entire route from 'a certain point in a field … Cae tri Bugail, and numbered 29 on the Parliamentary plan of the Newtown & Machynlleth Railway …' The Bill also sought powers to raise fresh capital, to enter into agreements with other railway companies 'in respect of the working, maintenance and use of the tramroad …', to convert the tramroad into a railway, to change the corporate name, to repeal clause 19 of the 1858 Act to permit the acquisition of land compulsorily and clause 20 to permit the use of locomotives. Charles B. Cooper, who appears to have worked primarily as a surveyor, signed the £50,000 estimate.

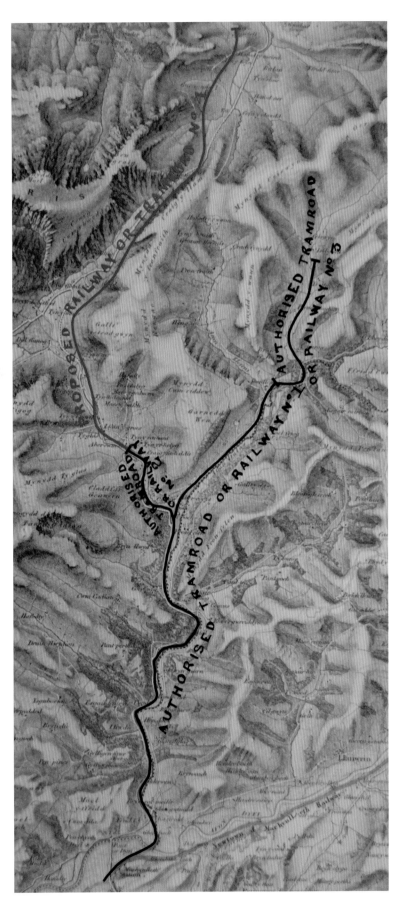

An extract from the plan deposited for the Tir Stent extension in 1863. (Parliamentary Archives)

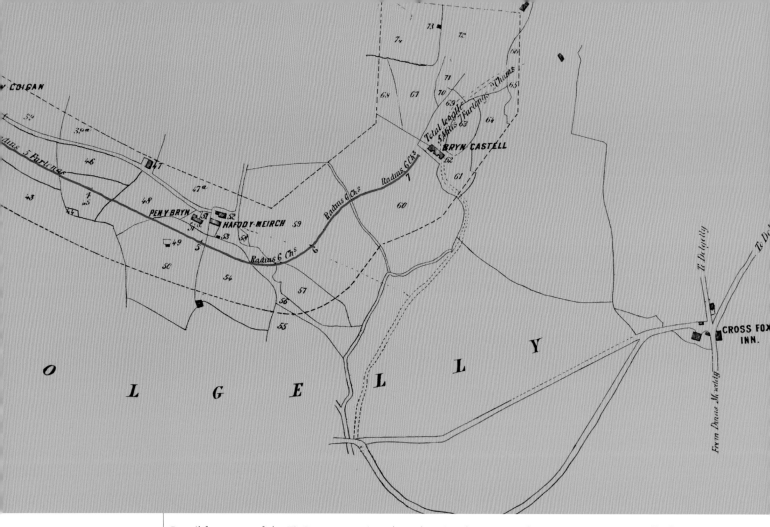

Detail from one of the Tir Stent extension plans showing the proposed terminus at Bryn Castell. There is no sign now that the land behind the farmhouse was once an industrial area.

Bryn Castell. The proposed Tir Stent extension would have terminated along the hedge line. The property takes its name from the tree-covered hill behind the house.

This Bill failed, although how much influence the Aberystwyth & Welsh Coast Railway directors' 8 January 1863 resolution to object to it had is unknown. Notice for another Bill, published under the name 'Corris Railway or Tramroad', was deposited in December 1863.

It sought powers to change the railway's name, 'to make and maintain' the existing three railways, to Aberllefenni, Tynyberth and Tycam, and a new railway, an extension from the Tynyberth line at Rognant to Bryn Castell, about a quarter of a mile from the Cross Foxes Inn road junction.

The Bill also sought powers to 'improve, alter, and straighten' the existing lines, to alter the gauge and to adapt them for the use of locomotives, and to 'cease to use … and … relinquish the construction of the tramroads made or authorized' between Machynlleth and Garreg, including the branch on the Penforddnewydd road, and to dispose of the land. The 1858 powers of construction had expired in 1862 so the clause regarding the Garreg abandonment leaves it unclear about just now much of it had been built.

The Bill's engineer was George Owen; he signed the estimate for £24,000. The AWCR petitioned against this bill too, withdrawing its objection on learning that its own contractor, Thomas Savin, had acquired control of the Corris, Machynlleth & River Dovey Tramroad and was willing to sell it to the AWCR. Without further objections the Bill was enacted on 25 July 1864.

Owen had been born in Tonbridge Wells, Kent, in 1829. Soon after the Bill was deposited he was appointed the Cambrian Railways' engineer, continuing to take other work at the same time. He shared with Benjamin Piercy, who became the engineer to the Cambrian Railways' constituents, the distinction of being apprenticed to Charles Mickleburgh the Montgomery estate agent and surveyor, and like Piercy, he also married one of Mickleburgh's daughters. His involvement with the Corris Railway

George Owen, the engineer for the 1864 Corris Railway Act, was appointed the Cambrian Railway's engineer on 14 September 1864, retiring from that position on 7 August 1897. He died on 5 May 1901 and was buried in Oswestry's public cemetery, his grave located in a prominent position by the entrance.

seems to have continued until his retirement in 1897.

With an additional £24,000 authorised capital and borrowing powers of £8,000, the 1864 Act sanctioned the four lines as described in the notice. 5 miles, 7 furlongs and 2 chains long, with two short tunnels, Railway No 4 was intended to carry iron ore from the Tir Stent mine. A report in the Welsh Mines Society newsletter (No 46) states that its output was to be routed via the Bala & Dolgelley railway, opened 1868, an option in 1864 that might explain the lack of interest in investing in the route to Corris. The output was later routed via an 18in gauge tramway to a wharf on the present A487 above the Cross Foxes Hotel.

With a gradient of 1 in 24 climbing from Tyddynyberth for five furlongs, followed by 1 in 62 for four miles rising to 674ft and then falling to the terminus at 1 in 46 for just over 1½ miles, the extension would have been difficult to work with horses, requiring extensive reconstruction

of the Tyddynyberth branch to improve clearances for locomotives. Features of the extension were two tunnels, 75 yards and 68 yards, on the 1 in 62 gradient, and a bridge across the turnpike.

The re-sanctioning of the existing lines was unusual; it was not included in the 1862 Bill. The 1864 Act's preamble explained the background. The company authorised in 1852 was referred to as 'the dissolved company' although the means by which it was dissolved were neither stated nor was it sanctioned by the Act. The 1858 company was identified as the existing company. The 1852 company had bought land that had been taken over and used by the 1858 company, it proclaimed, and although the two companies were 'the same or nearly the same' the land had not been vested in the 1858 company and 'it is expedient that [it] should be so vested'. It was perhaps to avoid any doubt that the 1858 company became the Corris Railway Company in the second clause.

It may also be significant that the definitions extended the word 'railway'

to 'include the tramroads of the company' to remove any uncertainty about the status of the branches. The 1852 company's property was transferred in clause No 4, the extension approved in No 8 and the use of steam locomotives at a maximum speed of 10mph in No 14. The Dovey branches were abandoned by clause No 26; the land not required there was to be sold within ten years. The abandonment had not been proposed in the 1862 Bill.

The railway was allowed to enter into agreements with the Oswestry & Newtown, Newtown & Machynlleth Railway and the Aberystwyth & Welsh Coast Railway. The preamble cited these and the Llanidloes & Newtown, Mid-Wales and Shrewsbury & Welshpool Railways as being directly or indirectly connected with the railway and seemed to say that existing powers in the AWCR Act of 1861 allowing agreements to be made between the AWCR and the second three would permit agreements between the Corris Railway and the second three also.

Contact with the wider world had been improved when the Newtown & Machynlleth Railway opened on 25 February 1863. On 23 July 1863, this company agreed terms for 'the Corris Tramroad Company' to have access to its Machynlleth station, and on 23 July 1864 sealed a conveyance to acquire some Corris land.

The Aberystwyth & Welsh Coast Railway's line between Machynlleth and Borth was opened on 1 July 1863, crossing the Garreg route at Machynlleth by a handsome stone arch. The lack of protective clauses in any of the AWCR's four Acts, however, had left the tramroad unable to protect its property. To make way for the AWCR between the tramroad and the river at Derwenlas the river had been diverted northwards, isolating the wharves and rendering the new arch superfluous.

Thomas Savin, the ambitious Oswestry-based merchant who was involved in the construction of most of the constituents of the Cambrian Railways, had probably acquired control of the railway in 1862, his participation most likely leading to the events that resulted in the 1864 Act. At the time of his bankruptcy in 1866 he had £13,000 of the company's £15,000 issued capital, 86.6%. Nothing is known of the circumstances of his acquisition; it would have entitled him to a directorship but no records survive to show this, except that the *North Wales Chronicle* reported that he had chaired the statutory company meeting held on 8 June 1864 to approve the Bill of the 1864 Act.

On 25 April 1864, the AWCR directors had resolved to buy the railway from him for what he had paid, only to change their minds the next day. From December 1864, they were pursuing a working agreement with the railway, then on 26 April 1865 resolved 'this company do purchase the Corris company for the sum of £21,000 payment to be made in preference shares of this company. That the debentures and

Seen in February 2018, this photograph shows the Penforddnewydd crossing of the Aberystwyth & Welsh Coast Railway. The Morben wharf branch was intended to run to the left of the road.

Poplar Terrace looking towards the standard gauge railway in 2018. The street followed the route of the line to Derwenlas.

The route to Derwenlas looking in the opposite direction.

all liabilities … be adopted … and that the additional rolling stock put on the line since it has been purchased by Mr Savin be taken from him at valuation.' Shortly to be merged into the Cambrian Railways, the AWCR said nothing more about the railway. Being tangled up in Savin's bankruptcy probably explains why the railway took no action to use its expensive new powers.

While Savin was still the principal shareholder, in May 1865 a 7-year-old child, David Evans, died when he fell from a wagon and was run over. Unknown to the driver, he had jumped on a wagon of a train running towards Derwenlas, near the AWCR overbridge at Machynlleth. The inquest jury returned a verdict of accidental death and recommended that 'Mr Savin, the proprietor of the line, should be respectfully requested to have the tramroad properly fenced in.'

Savin's involvement probably explains the comment in the preamble to the 1864 Act about the railway being 'connected directly or indirectly' with the six railways mentioned on page 36 and why it was a party to a scheme to amalgamate the Carnarvonshire, Nantlle and Beddgelert Railways with the Cambrian Railways in 1865-7. He had substantial shareholdings in the Cambrian and its constituent companies and in the Carnarvonshire Railway. Had the amalgamation bill deposited in December 1865 been successful, the restrictions on the railway's carriage of passengers and limiting its speed to 10mph would have been removed. The Cambrian resolved to withdraw the Bill on 26 April 1866. A second attempt in 1866 expanded the proposal to include the Brecon & Merthyr Tydfil Junction, Mid-Wales, Neath & Brecon, Swansea Vale, Potteries, Shrewsbury & North Wales, Pembroke & Tenby Railways, and the Llanelly Railway & Dock Company, and also failed to make the statute books.

Despite being authorised to use steam locomotives, the railway continued as before. The earliest information regarding its traffic comes from the Board of Trade's

annual returns for 1872, when 15,669 tons of slate was carried, earning £1,648. With operating expenditure of only £662 and a dividend of 5¾% perhaps the directors could see no reason to make changes. It had taken a while to get to this position though, for in 1867 the executors of Jane Causton, Causton's mother, had sued the company for the £500 Causton had lent to it against a mortgage deed in 1860. The debt had been repayable in 1863 but the company had been without funds, so it had been transferred to her on the understanding that it be repaid in 1866. She had died on 15 March 1866 and the debt was inherited by her executors, Causton and his siblings, along with her £2-3,000 estate. Their attempt to secure repayment when it matured on 25 September 1866 was unsuccessful.

Richard Greenhough (see bibliography) identifies William Lawrence Banks and Charles Miller Layton as directors in 1867/8. Both were involved with several railway companies, mainly in Wales and the Marches. They had interests in common with James Fraser, an accountant, another director and secretary from 1868 until 1871. According to C.P. Gasquoine (see Bibliography), Fraser also managed Savin's affairs in London.

Circumstances surrounding the death of three-month-old Ann Jane Owen on 27 February 1867 were similar to those of F.J. Ford in 1861. She fell into the river after the horse hauling her father's dog cart was startled by a sheep on the road near Esgairgeiliog and bolted. Her parents and the horse's trainer escaped, and she was rescued from the river by a passer-by but died later. The inquest jury blamed the turnpike trustees for not erecting a fence between the turnpike and the railway. No criticism was made of the use of a horse that was not fully broken in.

The outcome of a case brought against the railway by the Penegoes parish road surveyor at the Machynlleth petty sessions in 1868 unwittingly partially hinged upon Fraser's involvement. Section 116 of the General Turnpike Act of 1822 required the owners or occupiers of land adjoining turnpike roads to trim hedges to a height of 6ft and to prune trees, shrubs and bushes to prevent the road from being shaded, but no cutting or pruning could be ordered to take place between 30 September and 31 March. If there were no response to a surveyor's request for action within ten days he could apply to the justices for an order compelling the landowner to do the work or be penalised.

In this case, reported in the *Merionethshire Standard* on 6 June 1868, the railway's solicitor demonstrated that the summons was invalid because it had been issued out of season, on 23 February. Then, when it was produced it was noticed that it had been issued to 'J. Fraser' and not the company, causing the case to be dismissed because the summons had not been properly served. Nothing more was heard about the railway's hedge trimming liability.

Back on the railway, dissatisfaction with the lack of public facility was first expressed in the *Cambrian News* on 31 October 1873, a Corris resident complaining that if the 'miniature' railway had not been built a 'regularly gauged railway' would have been provided a long time ago, although the correspondent's displeasure had been increased by the lack of public access to the telegraph recently installed through the valley.

Nearly a year passed before further public agitation was demonstrated, by a meeting held on 27 May 1874, to call for 'proper locomotive railway accommodation' in the form of a railway between Machynlleth and Dolgellau, via Corris. The *Cambrian News* report of the meeting said 4ft gauge, surely an error for 4ft 8½in. If the Corris Railway Company declined to undertake this development, the meeting resolved, then an approach would be made to the Great Western Railway.

Just how much this meeting had any influence on the Corris directors there is no way of telling, but shortly afterwards a passenger service was started. The railway was quite open about this, returning 3,592 passengers carried 'in open trucks' for £90 income that year. On 6 October 1874 Fraser told the Cambrian's engineer, George Owen: 'We have started carrying passengers and goods up from Machynlleth to Corris and it is astonishing what a number will go up if we had any [sic] sufficient accommodation, as a beginning we would like to build a little warehouse and stable at Machynlleth and I am told that your company may be willing to let us have space at their yard for the purpose.' The increase to 11,830 passengers and £290 revenue in 1875 is indicative of the service being started part-way through 1874. Some rough arithmetic suggests that a fare of 6d was charged.

None of the local newspapers passed any comment on the new service, or the nature of the accommodation provided, except that a report on the new carriages delivered in 1878 contrasted them with the 'rickety, suffocating and dark boxes hitherto in use.'

As a goods-only line, the railway was beyond the interest of the railway inspectors and they must have been unaware of the note about passengers being carried in open trucks appearing in the Board of Trade's annual returns for several years. Accommodating passengers, however crudely, was regularising something that had probably gone on from the railway's earliest days, for a report in the *North Wales Chronicle* of 25 July 1860 gives a graphic description of a woman killed alighting from a moving train near the National School at Machynlleth on 11 July. 'The contractors for the conveyance of slates and flags … along the tramway allow their driver … to convey passengers occasionally down on top of the load for a "trifling consideration" …' The inquest jury, incidentally, instructed by the coroner to consider if the company's regulations and practices ensured the tramway's safe operation, whether the company allowed the conveyance of passengers, and whether it took any action to prevent its misuse on Sundays, returned a verdict of 'accidentally killed by having the right leg fractured by the wheel of a tram carriage'.

Fraser, based in London, admitted that he was unfamiliar with the location so maybe what he said to Owen should be treated with caution. The implication, however, is that slate was transhipped to the Cambrian with minimal facilities and that no other goods were being carried, even from Machynlleth. Unlikely as it may seem, it was to be 1877 before the railway reported the carriage of any merchandise, 818 tons for £157.

The Cambrian initially failed to understand that the Corris required accommodation close to its own tracks and not remote from them. On 13 April 1875 Owen reported to his directors that the warehouse was required to store 'grain, flour and other commodities' en route for Corris and the stable for 'feeding at mid-day the two horses that work the passenger trains to and from the quarries,

but these horses are stabled at the other end at night'. The Cambrian's works and traffic committee agreed to permit the erection of a warehouse and stable, subject to one month's notice for removal, on 28 January 1876. The rent was set at £2 guineas in 1878.

Although the railway's original facilities went unrecorded, some details are known of changes made on the quarries' behalf. Braich Goch required more space at Machynlleth in 1869, leading to the Cambrian to use old rail to extend its lower-yard siding at a cost of £60. When the Abercwmeiddau Slate Company applied for wharfage in 1876, the Cambrian's traffic manager was not convinced that the company needed the space requested, but after taking up credit references the following year the engineer submitted a proposal for a wharf 100ft long and 25ft wide that would cost £87 2s, the Cambrian also estimating the cost, £42, for extending the tramway, 'which should be defrayed by the quarry proprietors'. On 22 March 1877, the traffic manager recommended that the Cambrian pay for the wharf and the quarry company pay for extending the narrow-gauge siding to it. The quarry's name was often mis-spelled, incidentally, sometimes even on its own paperwork.

Aberllefenni plated its own wagons and several plates survive. One is in the railway's museum; this one is in a private collection. (Henry Noon)

CHAPTER 2

TRAMWAY COMPANY OWNERSHIP

The railway was brought out of its equine stupor in 1878, after it had changed hands twice in two years. Firstly, its share capital was acquired by the Tramways & General Works Company Limited, a company registered on 28 May 1877 with the objective of developing or modernising tramways; it already owned tramways in Middlesbrough, Dublin, Gloucester and Reading. Its owner, with £7,000 of £9,414 shares issued by 5 December 1877, was the Continental & General Tramway Company, which had built and owned the Hull Street Tramways. In 1871 one of Continental's founding directors had been Charles Edwards of Dolserau Hall, Dolgellau, which could provide a link to the interest in the Corris Railway. The identities of the vendors are unknown; they are most likely to have been the directors and Savin's inspectors.

The second transfer occurred in July 1878, when Transport & General's holding was sold to Imperial Tramways Company Limited, a company registered on 20 June 1878. On 17 July those companies and the Corris Railway Company made a legal agreement providing for the sale of its share capital to Imperial Tramways for £42,750. The agreement's preamble explained that the railway was unable to carry passengers, that it was desirable to relay the line between Machynlleth and Corris with steel rails and to provide proper rolling stock, that considerable expenditure would be required to execute such work and to provide sufficient rolling stock, and that the railway's capital was fully subscribed and the railway had no power to raise more capital or to borrow money. It would be 'a great advantage' to the railway and the shareholders that it should be used for the conveyance of passengers by steam locomotives and for authority to be obtained forthwith.

Payment was to be in the form of Imperial shares at par, £25,000 to be issued to Transport & General when the railway shares had been transferred to Imperial, within 28 days of signing the agreement. Beyond the sale, the contract contained some unusual requirements.

Imperial Tramways was to apply for powers to use the railway for the 'conveyance of passengers by steam locomotion' in the railway's name as soon as possible, and Transport & General was to contribute £600 towards the expenses. Transport & General undertook to pay Imperial a guarantee of 5% interest on the purchase price from 1 July 1878 until parliamentary authority had been obtained or 31 December 1880. Any company dividend of less than 5% would be offset against the guarantee. The company would pay its directors a total of £150 annually.

Within four months of the agreement being signed, Transport & General was to relay the track between Machynlleth and Corris with 44lb steel rail and enable the railway to satisfy the Board of Trade's requirements to permit the carriage of passengers with steam haulage 'at ordinary speed'. Transport & General would also pay up to £500 for any extra works required to meet any Board of Trade requirements specified before 31 October 1879. While the track was being relaid the railway was to provide 'all facilities' to the contractor so that traffic 'shall be interfered with as little as possible'.

The £17,750 outstanding from the purchase price was effectively the construction budget. When Imperial's engineer, Joseph Kincaid, had issued certificates for work done and equipment supplied, Imperial shares to the equivalent value were to be issued to Transport & General, less 5% retention. Any residual credit remaining in the construction account when the works had been completed was to be assigned to Transport & General in Imperial shares.

The agreement also called for the three steam locomotives and ten carriages ordered by Transport & General from the Hughes Locomotive & Tramway Engineering Works Limited of Loughborough, Leicestershire, to be taken over by Imperial Tramways for the railway's use. Established c1865, Hughes had also been recently registered, on 13 June 1877; the company's successors continue to trade with the rail industry from the same site.

Imperial's prospectus, seeking to raise £175,000, was issued on 18 July 1878. A preamble issued earlier explained that the five small systems were 'highly meritorious' but would benefit if their headquarters expenses were shared. The prospectus added that the dividend would not be dependent on the individual earnings of one system, which might vary, but on the profits of 'carefully selected undertakings'. Of the Corris Railway, it said that it was 'very similar to the well-known Festiniog line', served six quarries and had carried 20,751 tons of minerals and goods in 1877. The line was being relaid with steel rails to enable the company to take advantage of its powers to use steam haulage.

The table, compiled from the *Stock Exchange Year Book*, shows how the railway company's directors changed during the period of the takeover. John Marshall Gillies (chairman, London Tramways Company and director, Hughes Locomotive & Tramway), Joseph William Grieg (chairman, North Metropolitan Tramways Company), Alfred James Lambert (director, Transport & General and chairman, Hull Street Tramways Company) and W.R. Bacon (experience of UK and US tramways) were also Imperial directors.

Corris Railway Company Directors 1876-84

1876	1877	1878	1879	1880	1881	1882	1883	1884
J. Rowlands	J. Rowlands	J. Rowlands	J. Rowlands	J. Fraser	J. Fraser	W.R. Bacon	W.R. Bacon	A.J. Lambert
H.N. Hughes	J. Fraser	H.N. Hughes	J. Fraser	J.M. Gillies	J.M. Gillies	J. Fraser	J. Fraser	J. Fraser
J. Fraser	J. Garner	J. Fraser	J.M. Gillies	J.W. Greig	J.W. Greig	A.J. Lambert	A.J. Lambert	E.T. Gourley
J. Garner	C. Morrison	J. Garner	A.J. Lambert	A.J. Lambert	A.J. Lambert			W. Ward
C. Morrison		C. Morrison	C. Morrison	J.W. Maclure	J.W. Maclure			

Kincaid was also the railway's engineer. He became a member of the Institution of Civil Engineers in 1879, worked on many projects in the UK and overseas, and in 1891 was referenced by Bristol Tramways as its consultant engineer.

Another 1878 development had occurred in September, when the Cambrian's engineer, George Owen, reported to his directors that the railway required a strip of Cambrian land at Machynlleth to install a run-round loop. He justified approval as the railway would be a feeder to their company, as it already was.

Work on the ground was started in June, before the agreements were completed according to the *Cambrian News* (14 June 1878), which two weeks later said that tracklaying was started on 24 June. Completion of the re-railing, and construction of a station and engine shed at Corris, were reported on 13 September. The engine shed was actually located at Maespoeth, three-quarters of a mile south of the village, at the junction with the

Corris, with the 1878 station prominent to the right of the tree, with what appears to be a store shed alongside. (John Thomas)

Upper Corris branch, a handsome stone-built structure covering 2,016 square feet, large enough to stable three locomotives, with more than adequate headroom to allow boilers to be lifted when required, and space for a small machine shop and a forge. The contractor had been Bristol-based Mr Mosley or Moseley who, having completed his work, sold three horses, two carts and some timber at the Machynlleth fair on 18 September. Nothing more can be found about him.

It seems that the unofficial passenger train service resumed as soon as the re-railing was complete but did not meet the needs of all would-be users, who would try to make the journey to Machynlleth by taking wagons. Two men, Robert Evans, tailor, and David Morgan, stone mason, working in Corris and wishing to return home at around 8pm on 4 September 1878, did just that, but their 'train' ran away and derailed at speed near Pont y Coedwig. They had perhaps received some unwanted benefit from the newly relaid track. One of them was only slightly injured but the other broke an arm in two places. Reporting the incident, the *Cambrian News* said that it was fortunate that the accident had occurred when it did, because the 'ordinary passenger train', due at Corris at 8.30pm, was on its way up and had the men collided with it the result would have been fatal. 'The practice, of taking wagons, should certainly be put a stop to,' the newspaper declared.

As if this was not enough, some users of the passenger train also had cause for complaint if they were on the last train from Machynlleth on Saturday evening, the aforementioned 8.30pm presumably, a passenger writing to the *Cambrian News* (4 October 1878) that it had 'gained a notoriety for the disorderly conduct of its passengers. The filthy language and the curses uttered by drunken passengers are commingled with snatches of hymns and profane songs, together with tobacco smoke, which in close carriages is

This photograph might be of moderate quality, but it does reveal a good deal of information about Corris station not found elsewhere. On the left, the flag signals the presence of facilities for gentlemen. A similar flag at the far end, therefore, most likely indicates the presence of the ladies' facilities. The booking office window is adjacent to the second door on the left. Looking through the station, the signal box may be seen. What functions these five personnel performed is not known.

From 1879 Maespoeth was the railway's operational centre. This twentieth century view shows the signal box still in place, a stone building in front of the loco shed which had a room for stabling a pony, and a shed to the right of the loco shed door which might have been erected to store an out-of-use steam locomotive; here it is providing some shelter for one of the bogie carriages.

The Flood, Machynlleth

Machynlleth's Cambrian Railways station with the Corris Railway station behind it. Seen circa 1900, this image gives a good impression of the narrow gauge railway's first station's full extent. General Manager J.R. Dix has taken advantage of the different levels to promote the railway and its attractions by the simple, and cheap expedient of using the building's roof and some white paint. (Maglona Series)

unbearable. Respectable people prefer walking rather than be in such company.'

On 8 November, the same paper said that the Saturday-night behaviour was much improved. In future, it said, with the new carriages just delivered, passengers would have the luxury of first and second-class accommodation, well-lit and cushioned, a pleasing contrast. On 9 November the *Aberystwith Observer* added that the new carriages weighed about one ton, were 'constructed on the principle of the road tramway carriages' and the 1st class had cushions covered with green plush, adding that they were 'at present hauled by two horses, but ultimately a locomotive will be attached, when the road is complete and passed by the Government inspector.' There were six third class and four 1st class vehicles.

Two weeks later it reported that the new carriages were a boon to the passengers patronising the railway in 'this severe weather', speed much accelerated by the use of two horses instead of one. At Corris, it continued, the station was nearly complete, 66ft long, with booking office at

the village end, a platform under cover, a carriage shed and a goods shed alongside. Both platform and carriage shed benefitted from glazed roofs, and signal posts were also being erected. The latter were supplied by McKenzie & Holland, the Worcester-based supplier of signalling equipment to the railway industry. It was not possible for the Worcester-based firm Dutton & Co to have supplied this equipment, as postulated by the historian J.I.C. Boyd, as it was not established until 1889, although its founder, Edward Dutton, had previously worked for McKenzie & Holland.

The first of the locomotives had been delivered by the time the *Wrexham Guardian* had been published on 14 December, with the other two 'expected in a few days'.

As agreed, in December 1878 another Bill was deposited in Parliament. The only objector was Robert Davies Pryce, the Aberllefenni quarry owner. Living at Cyfronydd, near Welshpool, he had inherited the quarry from his mother. He was also a director of the Cambrian Railways and its chairman from 1884-6. Witnesses were heard in the Commons on

One of the four-wheeled tramcar-style carriages. No 'light gates' were ever fitted to the platforms of these vehicles, despite the undertaking given to the Board of Trade in 1880. (John Scott Morgan Collection)

The view from the Aberllefenni end of Corris station in August 1935, with one of the McKenzie & Holland signals still in situ. It had gone by 1947. (H.F. Wheeller)

Another signal is visible in this postcard view of Ffridd Gate crossing. The railway passed between the fence and the tollhouse. (Park, Newtown)

Ffridd Gate. No. 1.

Hughes 0-4-0ST No 3 and two tramcar-style carriages at Corris, c1880. A second-class carriage is next to the loco, the other is designated first-class.

8 May 1879. Pryce did not appear, neither did his barrister call any witnesses in his support.

The first witness was Joseph Richards Dix, the railway's general manager, who had taken up that position on 1 January 1879. Born in Nynehead, Somerset, in 1851, he was unusual amongst English managers of Welsh enterprises in that he settled in the community and learned Welsh, his marriage to Mary Elizabeth Savage, daughter of a Caersws grocer who doubled as the local registrar, on 15 January 1879 probably helping in that regard. His father's career with the GWR had taken his family to South Wales, before a transfer to the Cambrian Railways for appointments that included those of station master at Llanymynech and Machynlleth had taken it further north. Dix had started his railway career at Machynlleth and had been Newtown station master when appointed to the Corris Railway position.

He told the committee that he had been acquainted with the locality and the railway for the past seven years and that there were about twelve quarries served by the railway although they were not all working. Apart from experimental trips, the steam locomotives had not been used. He was familiar with the Festiniog Railway, knew that it carried passengers and ran at speeds higher than 10mph.

He thought that the carriage of passengers had started because it was not expressly excluded by the 1858 Act. When he joined the company, he discovered that the 1864 Act forbade it so he stopped it. Passengers had ridden in 'rude boxes; you could not call them carriages; only boxes with a door at each side'; he confirmed that the vehicles had roofs.

The population was dissatisfied with the withdrawal of the service, he explained, and people could not be deterred from riding on the wagons despite an omnibus service being started in substitution. It would be cheaper to carry the passengers by rail than by road. He did not anticipate running separate passenger trains but 'I suppose we should put a carriage on at the end of the mineral trains'. The quarrymen had asked for a workmen's train in the morning and in the evening.

His predecessor as manager had been David Owen, he said. Trains from the quarries, Aberllefenni was cited, were worked by quarry employees. Pryce could continue to work his own traffic if the railway was empowered to run passenger trains. The railway owned three or four wagons for its own purposes; the slate was carried in the quarries' own wagons.

Pryce's barrister had to be reminded that the railway already had powers to use locomotives and that there was no point in asking questions about them. There was some intensive questioning about the railway's proposed right to charge extra, 1d per mile, for the carriage of goods in its own vehicles and, despite the chairman's protestations, about the population of the district.

On the numbers who might be prepared to travel and being told that fifty people had complained about the passenger service being withdrawn, an incredulous barrister asked: 'Do you really mean to represent to the committee that there is any feeling at all in that part of the country that induced your board to ask Parliament to change the character of legislation simply to meet the requirements of the public on the grounds which you have stated, to meet the wants of the people who have complained?' But Dix was probably caught off guard by its verbose nature. 'I do not quite follow the question.'

Regarding the slate traffic, Dix said that Pryce's quarry, Braich Goch, currently sent a quarter of the railway's traffic, though perhaps only one sixth when all the quarries were working. Not unsurprisingly, he did not know how the locomotives were financed, or who paid for them.

The second witness was William Bright, manager of the Abercwmeiddau quarry for three years. He did not speak Welsh so relied on English-speaking shopkeepers for information about the locality. He was in favour of the railway carrying passengers: 'It would be a very great boon …' The quarry employed 120 men and produced 100-140 tons of slate in 28 days. It was a new quarry. Another 30 men would be employed shortly. Mr Spooner, 'one of the chief engineers in the neighbourhood', estimated that the quarry would be capable of producing 1,000 tons per month in three to four years. Charles Easton Spooner was the secretary and engineer of the Festiniog Railway Company who also undertook freelance work for quarries and railways in north Wales.

Responding to a question about traffic on market days Bright said that he had 'had to sit in an open carriage with just a piece of wood put across', which sounds indicative of riding on the railway. Shopkeepers wanted steam trains, their coal would be cheaper and the men would like to 'get down to their homes quicker on Saturday and back on Monday' – the quarrymen lived in barracks in the quarries during the week. He did not think that the railway was less fit than the FR for the carriage of passengers but, 'I know the Festiniog is a dangerous line to carry on, I should not like to go on it myself; it has such tremendous curves.' He had seen the trains at Portmadoc, he must have been told about the curves. Until a few weeks ago the quarry had hauled its own slate on the railway. Now the railway provided the horses and, using the quarry's own wagons, charged 3s per ton, a saving for the quarry.

The third witness was the vicar of Corris, the Reverend Robert John Edwards. He had been at Corris for three years and at Caernarfon previously. He and the residents had always expected the railway to adopt steam traction and carry passengers. He only knew of Pryce objecting. He had been a passenger 'pretty frequently'. He thought the cost would deter quarrymen from travelling daily even if they had the opportunity to do so.

Following an adjournment, on 9 May the committee concluded that the preamble had not been proved to its satisfaction. At a meeting of quarry owners held in Corris on 15 April 1880 reported in the *Cambrian*

News, 23 April, Pryce explained that he had opposed the Bill because it included 'a most insidious clause' giving the company power to change the rates and other purposes. The line was constructed solely for the slate traffic and he had thought it was his duty to oppose the Bill. There had been no time to consult the other proprietors and he had acted alone.

The company was not deterred, however, and deposited another Bill in November 1879. The Lords' committee resumed its examination on 9 February 1880, and, after hearing representations from the barristers, declared that it had become unopposed and could proceed. An unhappy Pryce and his quarry, Braich Goch, submitted petitions against it on 1 March. A petition in favour by 'inhabitants of Corris and other places' followed on 8 March and three days later another was submitted against it. Although this was presented in the name of 'Traders &c in district of Corris', it was Pryce's work too. In fact, there appears to be something rather odd about it, for the public meeting that he called to gather support for it was not held until 15 April and the meeting was aware that the select committee had decided that the petitioners had no *locus standi* on 11 March. Pryce told the meeting that if he had been able to represent more quarry owners he would have succeeded in overturning the Bill again. The royal assent was given on 9 July.

With the clause regarding rates removed, Pryce had justified his continued opposition to the Bill by telling the April meeting that he was concerned that the tramway proprietors might give the passenger traffic priority over the slate. An editorial in the 30 April 1880 issue of the *Cambrian News* gets to the root of his opposition, it seems. The carriage of passengers and the speedier operation of trains would not disadvantage him or his fellow proprietors, it said, but what he found irksome was that he had sold the land for four miles of the route for a nominal sum because it was going to be a mineral line. Now it would be used by passengers he thought he had not been paid enough and wanted more!

A letter in the same issue, incidentally, commented that the Corris Railway's average monthly goods tonnage was 1-1,500 tons, whereas on the Festiniog Railway it was 7-8,000. The latter also ran passenger trains, which clearly did not interfere with the goods traffic, so, 'how is it likely that passenger trains should interfere with goods traffic on the Corris line, where only a fifth part of the trade is transacted?'

After all the effort, the Act was quite short, only eleven clauses. The restrictions on speed and the carriage of passengers were removed subject to the company obtaining Board of Trade approval for any train that it wished to run at speeds greater than 15mph. For passengers, the company could charge a toll of 2d per mile plus an additional ½d per mile for any carried in carriages owned by the railway. The maximum charge, however, was 2d per mile for travel in a 1st or 2nd class carriage and 1d per mile for 3rd class travel. Were the toll and the charge to be amalgamated? Was the company expecting the operation of carriages that it did not own? The charges did not apply to special trains.

Pryce's opposition explains article 9, which obliged the company, if it carried passengers by steam or locomotive power, to carry 'the articles, matters and things' specified in the 1858 Act on the terms and conditions specified therein, provided the company was not obliged to find carriages or wagons for their conveyance.

A second paragraph said that unless the company conveyed such traffic by steam or locomotive power, or if it failed to convey it, it could not carry passengers in a manner that interfered with the 'owners or lessees of slates, slabs or minerals in the working of their traffic by means of horses, carriages and wagons as freely as they had been previously entitled'. Intriguingly, there is nothing in the previous acts that specifically allowed working the traffic to be devolved by the railway in this way although the 1858 Act's clause No 23, the 'power to take tolls', allowed up to 1d per

mile to be charged if the railway's own 'horse or other motive power' was used.

Dix's withdrawal of passenger services had been reported in the *Cambrian News* on 21 March 1879, saying that the company was running omnibuses between Machynlleth and 'Braich Goch junction', Corris, at the same times and with the same fares as before. There were, it said, three locomotives ready for work in 'the shed of the company at Corris' and the line was being fenced. (In December 1879 William Lloyd of Brynllwyd, Corris, succeeded with his claim for £7 for damage done by cattle getting onto his property through the railway's faulty fencing.)

The omnibus service becoming unprofitable after the end of the tourist season, however, it was withdrawn from 1 November 1879, reported the *Cambrian News* on 31 October. On 19 December, the paper reported that William Owen, landlord of the Braich Goch Inn, had started running a service of two return trips daily, in substitution, less frequently and therefore less capacity than the railway's service.

Imperial Tramways' directors' reports show that Transport & General paid £1,662 10s against the guarantee in 1879 and £2,190 4s 2d in 1880. The parliamentary delay had knocked holes into the contract so TGW had paid for the first Bill (1878) and Imperial had paid for the second. Including the cost of the 1880 Act, the railway's capital cost to Imperial had reached £43,984 2s 4d.

At Imperial's first general meeting, held on 30 December 1879, chairman A.J. Lambert explained that Corris traffic had been affected by competition from American slate and, when that had shown signs of abating, by a slate trade depression, going on to describe the situation regarding passengers and the failed Bill. In addition, he said, the quarry proprietors had tried to impose such onerous terms for haulage that the company had declined them, the steam engines remaining out of use for fifteen months as a result. However, steam services would be resumed on 1 January.

When news of the Bill's success reached Corris, any rejoicing was not universal. On 13 July, Morris Thomas, druggist of Corris, perhaps one of the shopkeepers who Bright said was in favour of the railway, wrote to the Board of Trade, asserting that a high wall separating it from the turnpike would be essential for public safety. The railway, he wrote, 'runs as close as 2ft to the other for a distance of about four miles and there is only a wire fence in some parts and a bare hedge for six months in the year in other parts of the line to hide it from view on the turnpike road. The railway traffic will therefore be so open to the turnpike road that with the many sharp curves on the line it must be highly dangerous to the gentry, the farmers and public generally travelling with horses on the turnpike road. Trusting you will deem the above worthy of your consideration.'

Responding, the company said that locomotives had been used for the goods traffic since the start of 1878, using the 1864 Act's powers, without any complaint, and there was not the 'slightest intention' of opening the line for passengers until the Board of Trade had given its approval. The date is in error for 1879; the correspondence was conducted with the secretary's office.

On 11 August 1880 Henry Sewell of Llwyngwern wrote that he and his family had to cross the railway on a level crossing 300 yards from his house, 'at which there is no person in charge. If the Corris Tramway is allowed to carry passengers by steam we shall be in danger of being run over in crossing the line as a train coming from Corris can only be seen a few yards off.' Saying that he had only recently moved into the area, he thought that there was no danger in using the crossing 'until the recent introduction of steam for working the line'. Sewell also complained about the proximity of the railway to the turnpike. He was told that the matter would be dealt with during the inspection.

The railway decided that it would be ready to start the passenger service on 19 September and gave one month's notice.

Before the inspection could take place, however, on 7 September John Evans of the Lion Hotel at Machynlleth told the Board of Trade of the hazards to be caused by the steam-hauled passenger trains. '… it will be extremely dangerous to my horses and conveyances and to the public generally going along the turnpike road …' In addition to being told that that matter would be dealt with by the inspector, Evans was also told that the commissioners or trustees of the toll had a remedy in clause 63 of the 1845 Railway Clauses Act, where if they thought that there was a risk of horses being frightened by steam locomotives they could apply to the Board of Trade for a certificate requiring the railway to erect a screen if such was found necessary.

The work being carried out on the railway obviously took longer than anticipated, for on 27 September 1880 notice was given that it would be ready for use by passenger trains from 30 September and be ready for inspection during the following ten days. Major Francis A. Marindin RE received his instructions the next day. The result could not have been as expected.

His report was submitted from Machynlleth on 7 October. A length of 5 miles 25 chains had been altered and improved for passenger traffic. It was intended to work with one engine in steam and 'the only passenger traffic expected was that of the slate quarry villages'. The width between tracks at passing places was 5ft. 44lb Vignoles-section, flat bottom, rail in 24ft lengths was fixed to half-round larch sleepers with dog spikes. The sleepers were 4ft 4in x 8in x 4¾in, laid 3ft apart. There was one spike fixed in each sleeper on each side, placed alternately inside and outside the rails. The ballast was broken slate waste and river gravel. He highlighted the steepest gradient of 1 in 35 and that there were several places with 2-chain check-railed curves.

In addition to the termini he noted intermediate stations at Pandy (Llwyngwern?) and Esgairgeiliog, saying that they had loops that were not used. Pandy was the only station without sidings. The 'mineral line junction' and 'engine shed siding' at Maespoeth were also noted. There were no overbridges, a 'timber viaduct' over the Dovey, and five bridges over streams, three with stone arches, one requiring repair. The single level crossing on a public road had 'proper gates, a lodge and signals'. There were three locomotives, four 1st class and six 2nd class four-wheeled carriages. The carriages had 3ft 8½in wheelbases, end doors and a brake.

Only Corris had a platform. Machynlleth had only a, 'bare shed, without any proper approach and with no urinals or conveniences.' The only building at intermediate stations was a signal hut. Corris had a covered shed and urinals but no separate accommodation for ladies.

There were features that he particularly did not like. Lineside structures, including walls, banks, houses, trees, signal posts and telegraph poles, were in 'a great number of places' between 1in and 6in of the side of the carriages and engine. The facing point locks were unsatisfactory. Fencing in some places was inadequate. For these reasons, he reported, the line could not be opened for passenger traffic without danger to the public.

Marindin went on: 'It is however altogether more of the nature of a steam tramway than a railway, the authorised speed being only 3 miles an hour more, and the rolling stock of a similar character, and before reporting as to the additional works which should be required I submit that the question should be referred for the joint consideration of the inspecting officers.'

There is no record of the railway's response to this bombshell. The track had been relaid, locomotives and carriages purchased, an Act of Parliament obtained and the inspector not only refused to approve the line for passengers but refused to issue any requirements, deferring to a committee of his colleagues.

Before drafting their report, the inspecting officers called for the reports of their predecessor, Captain Henry W. Tyler, of his inspection of the Festiniog Railway for passenger traffic in 1864. They were particularly concerned to know whether there were any deposited plans for the FR and what the sharpest authorised curves were. As the FR's 1832 Act pre-dated the requirement for such detailed plans and Tyler commented that the curves were as sharp as two and four chains there was no way of telling if they were intended by Parliament, or even by James Spooner, the line's engineer, in 1832.

The inspecting officers' report was compiled on 23 October 1880. In summary, they said that the railway could not be approved because of unauthorised sharp curves, the proposed use of 4-wheeled locomotives, the absence of clearances and insufficient space between the lines where they were double. The issue with four-coupled locomotives arose because of concerns about the loss of stability if an axle broke; the inspectors were obviously unaware of the four-coupled locomotives approved by Tyler on the FR. On 8 November, the Corris report was followed by a further 'postponement of opening' notice, this time with the recommendation that the company should withdraw its application to open the railway if the directors thought it unlikely that they could comply with the requirements within one month.

The company's rebuttal of the joint report was sent on 25 November 1880. While the directors recognised its technical validity, wrote the company's secretary from London, they believed special circumstances applied and the railway should be approved. Occasional trains would be run, comprising two cars and a locomotive. The cars were similar to those used on tramways and the speed would not exceed that already approved for steam tramways. The curves and gradients complained of were less severe than those found on tramways while the deeper flange allowed by the Corris rail and the check rails further diminished the risk of accident.

Four-wheeled locomotives had been approved for use on tramways and those used at Corris had been running without accident. Parallel tramlines were allowed to be only three feet apart, rather than the railway's 5ft. The limited clearances elsewhere were accommodated by not having opening windows. It was proposed to fit light gates to the carriage platforms to prevent anyone from putting themselves at danger. As the one engine in steam method of working would be adopted, the space at passing places was not relevant as the trains would not pass each other. Trains would be run as on a tramway, stopping as required by passengers and without having intermediate stations.

'In conclusion, I would add that in the event of your board sanctioning the carriage of passengers on the line as at present constructed, my directors will undertake to work it strictly in conformity with any regulations with which the board may see fit to couple their sanction.'

The inspecting officers made a joint response, sent on 6 December 1880. It pulled no punches: 'We submit 1st that as this railway was not constructed in accordance with the plans deposited for making it as a tramway, which plans only authorised curves of 5 chains radius. 2nd that as by Act of Parliament specially applied for, it has been transformed from a tramway to a railway, it is not, in our opinion, proper that the requirements deemed necessary to provide for the safety of the public travelling on railways should be departed from and therefore for the reasons stated in our memorandum of the 23rd October last, we cannot recommend the Board of Trade to sanction the opening of the Corris Railway for public traffic either as a railway or as a tramway.'

Beyond a formal acknowledgement, the railway appeared to make no response. Its official application to open the railway not having been withdrawn, the Board of Trade continued to send a notice of postponement each month, until eventually on 21 October 1881 it asked if the company would

withdraw the application until the railway was ready to be re-inspected.

Earlier, on 12 March, the inspecting officers had written, 'On the question respecting the Corris Railway, we see no reason whatever for altering the opinion in our minute of 6 December last. To deviate from it would be to afford a precedent, certain to be hereafter quoted when similar irregularities are introduced by the company constructing any new line.' There is nothing in the file to indicate what triggered this assertion. The notice was withdrawn on 2 November.

Kincaid, the engineer, wrote two letters on 18 January 1882, one to Marindin and one to the Board of Trade. He and Marindin had met and exchanged correspondence but the details were not recorded or retained. They had determined a strategy that Marindin thought would be accepted and now Kincaid had approval to make a commitment to the Board of Trade.

He undertook that all curves of less than five chains on the railway would be increased to five chains; all curves of five chains 'and under', a contradiction, would be check railed; a third pair of wheels would be fitted to the locomotives; a ladies waiting room would be provided at Corris and the platform width would be increased; at Machynlleth a ladies waiting room and approach from the main road would be provided; the space between double tracks would be increased to 6ft; facing points, other than those at the terminus, would be provided with patent locking apparatus, and obstructions on the eastern side of the railway would be removed so that none were closer than 2ft 4in at any point between 2ft 6in above rail height and the top of the highest carriage doors. Because it was impossible to improve clearances between the railway and the turnpike the fireman's side of the loco cab would be sealed; the same applied to the carriages.

This appeared to be satisfactory, Kincaid was informed, 'but the fitness of the line for passenger traffic must depend upon the report received from the inspecting officer.' Even now, getting the railway approved for passenger traffic was not going to be easy. On 3 July 1882 Kincaid wrote that the railway was ready to be inspected, the work having been carried out with one exception, the line's position between the river and road preventing the curve at Coedwig bridge from being increased to more than four chains. He hoped this would be acceptable.

Marindin returned to Corris and submitted his report from Shrewsbury on 18 July. He found that the requirements of 1880 had been met with the exception of the alterations to the curves. At Coedwig the curve was actually only 1.87 chains while five other curves the railway had said were five chains were actually 3.5 chains, 3.2 chains, 3.2 chains, 3.7 chains and 3 chains. Being told that this was owing to a miscalculation on the part of the agent who laid out the curves he 'therefore did not consider it to be necessary to proceed any further in my inspection'.

Receiving the news, Kincaid had an air of desperation when he wrote on 25 July 1882. 'Owing to a serious blunder made by the local engineer … many of the curves are under five chains … These curves as laid cannot be further improved and I should not have undertaken the works required to enlarge them to five chains radius had I not been misled …' He continued: 'Your requirements have been satisfied with the exception of the alteration of the curves and these have been improved to the utmost extent possible and I would submit that the Board of Trade having the power of permitting certain deviations from the parliamentary plans should not, in view of the narrowness of the gauge and the limited speed, refuse to sanction the opening of the line for public traffic, if the inspecting officer pronounces it, as laid, safe for passenger traffic.'

'My directors', he pleaded, 'would be quite prepared to affix to each engine a governor limiting the speed to any authorised maximum and to submit to any other regulations required … Seeing the great expense which the directors have incurred … that the inhabitants of the district are most desirous … that Parliament has sanctioned … my directors trust that you will see your way …'

It was to no avail. On 9 August, the Board of Trade informed Kincaid that permission could not be given because the curves were so much more tight than those approved by Parliament. In his note on Kincaid's letter, Marindin's colleague, Major General Charles Scrope Hutchinson, suggested that the company could apply for fresh powers authorising curves of not less than two chains with a requirement to use a governor restricting speeds to 10mph. He remarked that on the Festiniog Railway there were two-chain curves and the speed was 15mph and that there were steam tramways with curves as sharp as one chain operated at speeds of 8 or 10mph that had not been objected to. Marindin agreed with him.

There is no record of this strategy being communicated to Kincaid but on 19 October he wrote that he had been instructed to prepare an application to Parliament and wished to know if the Board of Trade had any objection to this stratagem. He was informed that there would be none provided there were no curves of less than two chains and that the speed of trains was mechanically governed to 12mph.

The Bill was deposited in December 1882. While it was being processed the Board of Trade became concerned about two level crossings that had not been authorised. Although it decided that no further action was required, so missing the opportunity of having them validated by Parliament, their status was to be raised later. The Act received the royal assent on 18 June 1883.

By its terms, the Board of Trade was authorised to approve the works for the 'conveyance of passengers notwithstanding that the same may not have been constructed in some respects in accordance with the deposited plans relating thereto …' subject to the minimum curvature being two chains and the speed limited to 12mph unless otherwise permitted.

Dated 28 November 1883, Dix's plan for the stations at Esgairgeiliog and Llwyngwern served both sites. The staff had a small office with fireplace while passengers were provided with a bench seat in an open alcove. (National Archives)

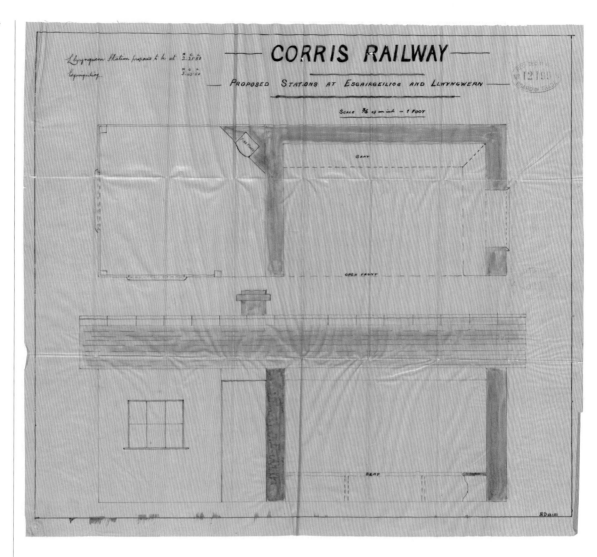

Marindin was instructed to return to Corris on 23 June 1883 and submitted his report in London on 5 July. The permanent way was unchanged from 1880, the curves had been altered and complied with the 1883 Act. 'The engine in use is also fitted with a mechanical apparatus which prevents it from running at a higher rate of speed than 12mph.' The intermediate stations had been removed. There were two level crossings on public roads, one of which had been a private road in 1880. The crossings were provided with gates and lodges, one was interlocked with signals, the other required discs and lamps attaching to the gates and a signal controlled by the keeper. With these requirements, and the fitting of the other two locomotives with governors, Marindin wrote that, 'upon the receipt of a satisfactory undertaking as to the method of working with one engine only in steam, the opening of this single line for passenger traffic may be sanctioned.'

The undertaking was made the next day. It had taken nearly three years, three inspections and an Act of Parliament to get the railway approved for the carriage of passengers. So much for the agreement's four months. No doubt the directors, and Imperial Tramways, would have appreciated Transport & General Work's 'additional works' £500 if they had still been able to call upon it. 20,162 passengers were carried during the remainder of 1883, a figure that doubled the following year.

Within a few months of opening, the company had reconsidered its position concerning intermediate stations and thought it should provide at least a shelter

at Esgairgeiliog and Llwyngwern. On 26 October George Owen, the engineer, had written to the company that he, 'cannot see that any difficulty should arise from the Board of Trade upon the company giving an undertaking to put up sufficient shelter by erecting waiting sheds. No platforms will be required and signalling is all that can be desired.' His letter was passed to the Board of Trade which consulted Marindin, who said that either the company should submit plans for approval or that it should construct the stations and submit them for inspection.

A plan was submitted on 11 December 1883, with a note explaining that Llwyngwern was on a gradient of 1 in 157 and a curve of 21.52 chains to the left, from Machynlleth, and Esgairgeiliog was on a gradient of 1 in 187 and on a curve of 13.53 chains, also to the left. Marindin decided that the buildings could be erected without the need for loops or platforms but that the company should

'provide the usual sanitary conveniences, which judging from the plans … have not been thought of'. He also required an inspection.

Apart from painting, delayed because of the weather, the stations were ready for Marindin by 26 February 1884. He reported from Shrewsbury on 6 March. Esgairgeiliog had a siding facing down trains. The signalling was satisfactory and, 'sufficient accommodation has been provided for the class of traffic on this narrow gauge line,' he wrote, which nicely escapes the point of whether these wayside stations had been provided with 'the usual sanitary conveniences'. Nameboards were required and had been ordered; on the understanding that they would be 'at once supplied' he could recommend that use of the stations be sanctioned. The *Aberystwyth Observer* reported that the stations were opened on 6 March, immediately after Marindin's inspection.

Esgairgeiliog c1890. A ventilated goods van is stabled in the siding. (John Thomas)

A later view of Esgairgeiliog station, with the original timber office portion replaced by stone. The private branch on the right served the Era quarry. Although it was not railway property, the railway became caught up in a dispute over the use of the bridge where it crossed the river.

A train arrives at Llwyngwern in the 1890s. Three of the four carriages comprised two four-wheel carriage bodies placed on bogie underframes. To the left of the nameboard an old van is in use as a store. Some protection has been provided for the engine crew when running chimney first.

Home time for quarrymen at Llwyngwern. Either the old van has been replaced by a shed or it has been clad to provide further protection from the elements.

A passenger train arrives at Llwyngwern towards the end of the nineteenth century. The private branch line on the right served Llwyngwern quarry. (Martin Fuller collection)

During the three years it had taken to secure approval for passenger trains, the operation of other services had not been without difficulty. On 13 March 1882, the railway had sued William Robinson, a carrier, for £7 12s 6d at Dolgelley county court. The sum related to 305 loads of building stone taken from Gaewern and Braich Goch at 6d per load. Robinson counter-claimed £4 for damage sustained to his cart when passing over rails in the road.

Dix said that Robinson had declared only 71 loads but the Braich Goch clerk had recorded another 305. Under examination, however, the clerk said that he could not say how many loads had been taken by road and how many by rail. Robinson then admitted to 120 loads going by rail and the judge allowed £2 for damage to the cart, awarding £1 and costs to the railway.

Although it was in the name of the Braich Goch Slate Quarry Company, Pryce was responsible for another case brought by the railway and heard in the High Court Queen's Bench Division on 5 December. He had objected to being charged for returning empty wagons to the quarry, an issue that had not been subject to a legal decision. Braich Goch slate was transported 5¼ miles in its own wagons, using its own haulage, paying 1s 3¾d per ton, equating to the maximum 3d per ton per mile allowed by the 1858 Act. Its own haulage was also used to return the wagons to the quarry.

The railway's barrister's argument that the railway provided a service, and was entitled to a payment for it even though its statutes were quiet on the subject, found no favour with the judges, one of whom asserted that after the slate had reached Machynlleth the railway rendered no service. It signals the wagons back and its rails were subject to wear, which cost just as much as the hauling, the barrister submitted, but to no avail. After some legal argument touching on other cases, the judges found in Braich Goch's favour, with costs, without hearing its defence.

The *Cambrian News*, 8 December 1882, commented, 'Railway companies are always trying to kill traffic by extraordinary charges. This important decision will be received with interest in many parts of the district.'

The operation of regular passenger services brought an extra benefit for the railway and the locality from 1 November 1883, when the General Post Office started using the railway to transmit the mail. Letters would be received an hour earlier and sent an hour later than when road transport was used. Mail for the Talyllyn area was also routed through Corris, instead of via Towyn and Abergynolwyn, reported the *Cambrian News* on 26 October. Taking advantage of the gradient, the railway ran a mail wagon from Corris at 5.30pm each day, the wagon being returned attached to a passenger train the next day.

Another court case resulted in Thomas Pugh, Pantperthog, being awarded £6 in respect of a pig run down by a train at Machynlleth county court on 15 February 1884, his argument that a loose gatepost had allowed the pig to get onto the railway being accepted by the court.

Improved access for passengers transferring between the stations at Machynlleth was agreed by the Cambrian Railway's traffic and works committee on 30 July 1884. The traffic committee had reported that, 'the Corris company are anxious to have a flight of steps provided between the two companies at Machynlleth. At present passengers have to get off the end of the platform, pass across some of the company's sidings, which, under cover of darkness, is very dangerous. The cost of providing suitable steps is estimated by the engineer at £20, and of this the Corris company would be willing to contribute one half.' The steps, 31 and a 16ft rise, were in place by 18 August 1884.

In 1884, Imperial's capital expenditure was restated to include the reference to the railway's capital being purchased for £25,000 already mentioned. £1,239 5s 4d had been spent to meet the requirements for passenger traffic and £610 17s 3d on

Parliamentary and engineering expenses, of which £200 was written off. Post-purchase expenditure came to £8,102 19s 5d. Even taking the guarantee payments into account the restated figures do not balance with the £42,750 purchase price first given.

Deposited sets of directors' reports for the railway are incomplete before 1885. Coincidentally, the earliest surviving minute book also dates from that year, when the directors were Lambert, Fraser, William Ward and Colonel Edward Temperley Gourley. The first was the chairman. Gourley, a ship owner and MP for Sunderland, and Ward had joined the board in 1883 and 1884 respectively. Ward was probably a promoter of the Portsmouth (Kingston, Fratton & Southsea) Tramways Company but this has not been confirmed. The secretary, Edward Miall Fraser, had been in office since 1871, except for 1881/2, and had conducted the correspondence with the Board of Trade after Kincaid ceased to be involved during 1883; he was James Fraser's son.

The directors' meetings were held in London at about two-weekly intervals with Dix occasionally in attendance. After reviewing the financial position, the directors would deal with correspondence, mostly from Dix. Some of the meetings had only one or two items to deal with and must have been very short.

It would be reasonable to expect some formal structure to have been put in place to reimburse Imperial Tramways with the costs it incurred on the railway's behalf. No advantage was taken of the 1864 Act's authorised but unissued capital, in 1885 the company deemed the authority expired, and the opportunities offered by the 1880 and 1883 Acts were not taken. Notwithstanding, payments to Imperial were made at irregular intervals, presumably for management services and when the directors thought the railway could stand it; £450 was paid in 1885/6. There is no obvious correlation between these payments and entries in Imperial's accounts.

The accounting was not straightforward. The half-year to 30 June 1885 was not typical but serves as an example. On the capital account £40 had been spent on new rolling stock and £260 17s 3d had been written off at 31 December 1864. On the revenue account, a £450 (6% on £15,000) dividend had been received and the £260 17s 3d deducted. The balance sheet showed £143 8s 5d owed by the railway as a liability.

The Board of Trade returns show that during the last seven years of horse haulage an average of nearly 17,000 tons of slate had produced dividends ranging from 4½% to 8½%. There were no dividends in 1879 and 1880, while for the following seven years a slightly reduced slate volume and passenger traffic from 1883 produced dividends in the range of 1⅛% to 5%.

Even with the steam locomotives in use, the railway had not turned its back on horse haulage, because the locomotives did not venture onto the branches. In some cases the quarries continued to undertake their own haulage and in others they paid the railway for it. On 8 May 1885, the directors dealt with a notice from Abercwmeiddau terminating the company's haulage of its slate. A week later Dix was authorised to negotiate to undertake Braich Goch's haulage for 2s per ton with a rebate of 1s per ton on any excess over 5,000 tons carried in six months. Over the years there were regular entries relating to horses, their equipment and accommodation in the reports, where the expenditure was allocated to capital. On 27 August 1885, the directors approved Dix's request to buy a new horse for £30 and to sell one that was 'past work'. In December, 'the horse employed at Machynlleth station had cut its foot severely but was now recovering.'

It was November 1885 before any progress was made over the haulage. Braich Goch declined to pay 2s per ton while Abercwmeiddau agreed to pay 2s 6d and to oil their own wagons. The latter, however, wished to have the terms embodied in an agreement but the directors resolved 'that no departure be made from the existing custom'; the arrears were settled at the end of the month. Dix was to continue negotiating with Braich Goch.

There was bound to be conflict with the quarries allowed to undertake their own haulage and this came to a head in January 1887. Dix complained that, 'trains were frequently delayed by the irregularity of the Braich Goch Company's trains and that their manager claimed to have the use of the line for two hours in the mornings and two hours in the afternoons.' Unlikely as it seems, a timetable for August 1887 reproduced in Boyd (see bibliography) shows no advertised train movements between the arrival of the 9.45am from Machynlleth at Corris at 10.10am and its departure at 12.50pm and again after that train returned at 2.00pm until 4.40pm. Braich Goch's rights were to be investigated.

Early in 1887 Dix obtained a patent for a device intended to prevent locomotives' wheels from slipping by using a jet of steam. On 5 May the directors agreed that he could equip the locomotives with it and to pay him a royalty of £1 per locomotive per annum. In theory, using steam had advantages over the sand used hitherto, in that it was always available, not subject to

clogging the pipes and would not damage the motion. It might be assumed that in practice the device was not effective as it did not remain in use.

Another station was being considered in April 1885, when Dix reported that he had been negotiating for the small piece of land required at Fridd Gate. The owner was seeking £5 annually for the land and the adjacent house the crossing keeper was using. Dix was instructed to get the best price, and to get the house rent free for a year if the railway put it into good repair. Trains stopped there from 2 October and earned £3 0s 9d during the first month. The Board of Trade was not troubled on this occasion.

The railway was also required to be kept in good repair and a programme of re-sleepering was in place in the mid-1880s. Whether this means that the steel rails installed in 1879/80 had been laid on old sleepers or sleepers installed then had not lasted well is not known. The engineer, George Owen, inspected the line annually and reported on the areas that needed attention. In March 1885 Dix reported that

No 3 passing Fridd Gate in April 1948.

he had sourced 5,000 larch sleepers for the main line at 1s each and 1,000 for the branches at 9d. In June he estimated £900 expenditure on sleepers and had ordered £100 worth. On 31 July he reported delivery of '800 out of the first 2,000 large sleepers' at a cost of £40. Gourley visited the railway in September and recommended that 'square creosoted sleepers' should be used on curves, at joints and in the middle of each rail length, also that a trial should be made of using galvanised and tarred spikes. Imperial allocated £100 for expenditure on sleepers during the second half of the year.

In May 1886 the section between Llwyngwern and Esgairgeiliog, about 1½ miles, was reported to be complete and there were 1,000 sleepers in stock. By July half the line, 1,100 yards from Machynlleth, 2,300 yards from milepost 2, and 500 yards at Corris, would have been completed when the 650 sleepers in stock had been used. Faced with this information Dix was instructed to, 'limit expenditure under all heads to what is absolutely necessary for the safe passage of the traffic.' Dix reported the task complete except for 150 yards on 27 November 1888. Five hundred sleepers were still required for the sidings at Machynlleth, Maespoeth and Corris.

With regards to rolling stock, in March 1885 Dix had reported discussions with the Falcon Works at Loughborough with a view to modifying the brake van for use on mineral as well as passenger trains. This was probably changes to its couplings and might explain the £40 spent by Imperial on otherwise unaccounted for new rolling stock already mentioned.

The railway was no different to any other when it came to passengers or local youth misbehaving. In June 1885 a passenger, Griffith Edwards, was brought to the directors' attention for jumping from a train in motion and on another occasion for wounding a sheep and driving it onto railway premises. In July Dix reported that Edwards had been fined 1s and £1 10s costs. Dix was to have posters printed announcing the conviction and to exhibit them at stations.

More seriously, in May 1886 Owen Griffiths, aged 11, was killed when a wagon fell on him after he and four others got into two wagons on the Upper Corris branch and set them in motion. They derailed and went over the embankment near Braich Goch. Joseph Hughes, a postman, broke his leg. Bringing a verdict of accidental death, the coroner's jury recommended that wagons should not be left unattended. The directors resolved that 'if possible' the wheels of wagons left on the line should be secured by a chain and lock.

The police were not above misusing the railway either. Reported on 3 June 1886, Sergeant Roberts 'borrowed' a wagon from Aberllefenni and travelled in it to Corris. Dix reported it to the chief constable but 'did not think it advisable to take further action', a position the directors agreed with.

Staff also got into trouble. A platelayer was dismissed in October 1885 after he had been acting as signalman at Machynlleth and derailed a passenger train. Viewing with a twenty-first century perspective, the author wonders if he had been properly trained. If it was a train in service, which was implied, then the Board of Trade should have been informed. In November 1888, a trolley ran away at Maespoeth bank, smashing the gates at Pont Ifans and damaging those at Llwyngwern before it stopped at Fridd Gate. The two men who were using it were sacked.

More seriously in the directors' eyes, in December 1888 Dix detected that E.W. Evans, station master at Esgairgeiliog, had received money without accounting for it on two occasions. The money was paid in and he 'severely reprimanded' Evans. The directors resolved that, 'the manager be informed that the board take a serious view of such delinquency and had the circumstances been reported earlier would have directed the dismissal of Evans.'

The Talyllyn Railway had been opened between Towyn and Abergynolwyn to serve the Bryn Eglwys quarries in 1866.

The quarries were working the same slate veins as those around Corris, about four miles distance in a straight line, and the two railways shared the same 2ft 3in gauge. In November 1885 William McConnel, then chairman of the TR, 'inquired the price of the spare engine'; Dix was instructed to say that it would not be sold for less than the original price, £700.

The reference to 'the spare engine' suggests that the railway's traffic did not require three locomotives in traffic, which the method of working, one engine in steam, and the contemporary timetables tend to support. It is most likely that normally one engine would have been in service while another was undergoing routine maintenance. It would only have been on rare occasions, holidays perhaps, that the weight of a train would have required two engines and then they would have been double-headed. It was to be 1951 before the TR received any 'spare' engines from the Corris Railway. In the meantime it made do with two it had been equipped with in 1865/6.

There are no records surviving that deal with the disposal of the unwanted formation to Derwenlas and Morben. When the Machynlleth district highways board wanted to extend its footpath from the town to the Dovey river bridge through the narrow-gauge arch under the Cambrian line to Aberystwyth in November 1885 it approached the Cambrian for permission. The railway should have had a good stock of spare rail arising from the abandonment, albeit only suitable for use on the branches.

Travellers reacted to the railway experience in different ways, the contributor of a piece of doggerel describing a Welsh tour published in the *Warrington & Mid Cheshire Examiner* in August 1886 saying merely that the experience was 'a rum do'.

In contrast, a passenger who signed himself 'Dulas' wrote to the *Cambrian News*, 10 September 1886, calling for travelling to be made 'tolerably comfortable', saying, 'The carriages are light and airy, affording a fine view of the winding Dulas valley. But whatever pleasure is obtained in that way is utterly marred and destroyed by the intolerable constant shaking of the train, the indescribable noise by which no conversation can at all be carried on while the train moves.' While other railways were vying with each other to improve passenger conditions, the Corris company, which endeavoured to attract tourists, was fifty years behind the times, he said.

The trains were slow, the carriages unsprung and there were no buffers between them. The seats were made from narrow wooden slats spaced about an inch apart which allowed cold air through, 'and it is reported many [have] suffered in health thereby.' He wished the company not to think about its pockets but to do something for the comfort of its customers. If nothing was done then a boycott would be a powerful tool.

The following week, 'Corrisian' wrote that Dulas's remarks were fabrications, made not in the public interest but out of personal ambition or malice. The carriages, he declared, were 'universally praised for their ease and comfort', they were sprung and equipped with buffers, and some vibration had to be expected, even at low speeds. The company, he concluded, deserved the public's appreciation and thanks for, 'the efficient manner in which this difficult undertaking is conducted, it is undoubtedly the greatest boon of the age to our neighbourhood.' If Dix did not have a hand in this response then he must have known who did.

On 27 December 1886 though, 'Ajax' wrote to say that not only did he agree with Dulas but that it was scandalous for the railway to only offer two classes, 1st and 3rd, of travel. He had travelled from Corris the previous week and at Esgairgeiliog the train had been joined by some workmen. He was amazed at their conduct, entering the compartment in a rough manner and wearing dirty clothes. At Machynlleth someone drew his attention to the state of his own clothing, caused by the workman sitting next to him. The railway should have three classes and attach a carriage for the workmen to the 4.25pm train, and the 12.40pm on Saturday.

The weather and the consequences of it proved to be an ongoing problem for the railway. On three days over the winter of 1885/6 trains were stopped by flooding at Machynlleth, 3ft 6in above the track on one occasion. During the same period, a landslip also occurred at Coedwig curve and the retaining walls at milepost 3 and Pont Ifans required attention in April 1886. Dix estimated £40 to repair them but the directors wanted him to see if buttresses or timber shoring would be a more economical solution – he had them pulled down and rebuilt.

Another storm on 15 October 1886 brought down 35 yards of embankment and retaining wall between Llwyngwern and Esgairgeiliog. The minutes reveal a conflict between Dix and engineer Owen on a remedy, the former reporting that it would take two weeks to repair and that trains were stopped in the meantime, the latter recommending a new wall on deeper foundations 'than the manager considered necessary and that he [Owen] must disclaim any responsibility for the stability of the work'. Dix was instructed to confer with Owen and to follow his instructions. After the secretary and Owen inspected the site on 27 October the latter said he was, 'thoroughly satisfied with the way in which the work … had been carried out.' The line was reopened on 3 November.

It is indicative of the fluctuating nature of the slate quarrying industry that the railway sometimes had problems getting paid and would resort to direct action to protect its interests. Two quarries made regular appearances in the minutes, Abercorris and Abercwmeiddau. In December 1885, the Abercorris company was £56 9s 9d in arrears, accumulated over six months. When one of its cheques was returned unpaid in July 1886 Dix was told to detain seven wagons loaded with slate. He seized another at Machynlleth

when the quarry closed 'for want of funds' in November and owed £31 5s 7d; the Cambrian seized a wagon as well. In January 1887 Dix was told to demand cash for any haulage until the debt was settled. When Abercorris's liquidator demanded the wagon's return a few weeks later Dix told him that it had been taken before his, the liquidator's, appointment and stated that it would not be returned until the debt was cleared. In November 1887 Dix asked the directors for permission to use the wagon; he was told to ensure that the railway retained possession of it.

By February 1886 poor trading had forced the closure of Abercwmeiddau; it had been in arrears for some time and Dix had been insisting on cash in advance for several months; £63 5s 7d of the arrears was paid in June 1886 and the quarry reopened in August.

In January 1886, Dix had been concerned about the loss of benefit for the railway when he learned that photographs of Talyllyn displayed in the Cambrian Railways' 1st class carriages described the lake as being 'near Towyn'. His action in asking for the caption to be changed to 'near Corris via Machynlleth' was approved by the directors but he was advised 'to adopt a more conciliatory tone when dealing with Mr Conacher', the Cambrian's secretary. By April he had obtained approval to display advertising boards at twelve of the Cambrian's principal stations on the coast.

Dix was concerned about the route to Talyllyn and Cader Idris being misrepresented because from July 1885 he had been promoting, via advertisements in the *Cambrian News*, Machynlleth and Corris as the best route, offering special fares. In June 1886 he told the directors 'he had been offered a suitable brake for the Talyllyn lake traffic for £20'. With their agreement arrangements were put in place, and from 2 July the advertisements were changed to include a line reading, 'A coach runs twice daily from Corris along the side of the lake to Talyllyn.'

Talyllyn, the destination for Corris Railway coach services. With some modifications, the buildings form part of the Ty'n y Cornel Hotel complex. The lake feeds the Afon Dysyni which flows into Cardigan Bay north of Tywyn.

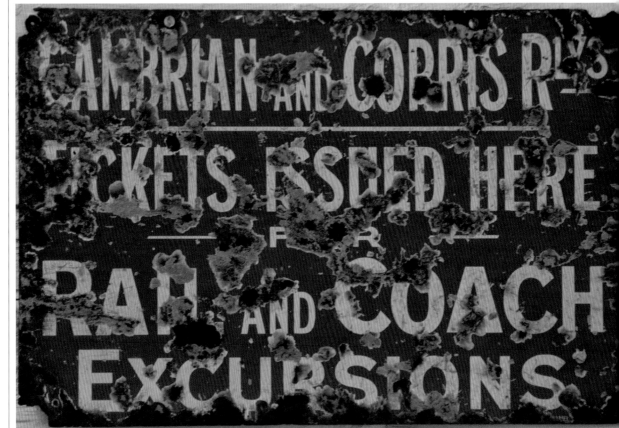

An enamel sign on display in the Corris Railway museum.

Two of the coaches at the eastern end of Talyllyn. (Donald George)

At the head of the lake a coach driver and his steeds rest while the passengers take refreshments. (Donald George)

Two of the coaches, plus staff and villagers, pose for a photograph in Corris. (W.H.A. Edwards)

At the end of the season Dix reported that the 'Talyllyn car' had carried 1,019 passengers and earned £46 15s 9d since 1 July. In addition to the £20 cost of the brake, the harness had cost 10s. A second horse was bought for £15 and sold for £12. The cost of the first was not recorded. In April 1887, he bought 'a car suited to the Talyllyn service' for £18.

Traffic figures included in the reports from 1890 reveal that the railway ran two road services: posting, the hire of horses to travellers, and the Talyllyn coach operation. With a return journey of eleven miles, the latter was always the more popular of the

two, with numbers carried ranging from 1,989 in 1891 to 9,226 in 1902. Posting bookings ranged from 316 in 1890 to 1,068 in 1900.

Back in 1885, the Corris postmaster, Griffith Edwards, was prosecuted at Towyn for leaving a train in motion at Fridd Gate. Producing the regulations, Dix said that he did not wish to press the case but to stop the practice. Edwards was fined 1s and costs.

Technology in the form of a Byng telephone system was installed between Dix's office and 'the station' in June 1886. It cost £3 18s 6d. The office was at Dix's house, originally close to the station at Arddol Terrace in Bridge Street, Corris, and later a larger property on the edge of the village.

Transhipment of coal from rail to road at Corris could be avoided if wagons were dragged over the road to the customer's premises. Meeting on 25 April 1885, the highway board had got wind of this practice, resolving to inform Dix that not only was it forbidden but that the company would be liable for any damage done. On 18 July however, it gave permission for the railway 'to take trains along the roads at Corris for delivering coal', on trial, on payment of £1 a year.

But by 22 May 1886 the board seems to have had a collective lapse of memory, for its clerk was directed to inform the railway that unless it 'ceased trains over the roads' proceedings would be taken. Following a public meeting to debate the issue in September, the railway was allowed to continue the practice. The directors, 'resolved that the manager be informed of the satisfaction of the board at the result of his exertions.'

Nevertheless, the issue obviously continued to raise tensions in some quarters, for on 7 January 1887 two cases were brought against railway employees at Towyn petty sessions. In the first, the police accused Edward Thomas of 'causing injury or damage to the highway' contrary to the terms of the Highways Act of 1835 at Bridge Street, Corris, on 20 September 1886. The railway's counsel argued that the railway's Act justified the use, there

was no evidence of damage, wagons were taken on the roads as a convenience for the public and, with the exception of some individuals who had moved into the area recently, the inhabitants did not object. The case was dismissed, the magistrates saying that the alleged offence had not been contemplated by the Act of Parliament under which the summons had been issued.

In the second case, Edward Thomas (again) and Hugh Thomas were charged with having used 'trams' on the roads with projections, the wheel flanges, contrary to bylaws, on 3 January. Counsel argued that the bylaws were unreasonable and could not remove a right created by Parliament and the flanges were not projections within the bylaws' meaning. Perhaps tiring at the 'very long legal argument' the bench dismissed the case, adding that if bylaws were to be enforced, proceedings should be initiated by the authority which made them.

The *North Wales Chronicle* of 15 January 1887 reported that public support for the railway's position was demonstrated on

the evening after the hearings by Dix being carried through the streets of Corris. The minutes of 13 January had noted that, 'the people in the village [are] subscribing to defray the company's expenses.' It might have been more productive if the highways board had simply billed the railway for any damage done. On 7 May, the sanitary inspector reported that installing drainage at Corris would be impracticable until the roads were improved, and that was impossible while 'trams' were allowed to go over them.

Lambert, the chairman, and Ward had visited the railway on 17/18 September 1886. They reported, 'The widening of the line between Corris and Aberllefenny was in course of completion and it had been proposed to put down steel rails with the view of extending the passenger traffic to Aberllefenny. One of the engines needed repairs and a bogie was required for the third engine. Some new cars were wanted and those in use required overhauling.'

There had been no resolution about extending passenger services to Aberllefenni. Lambert was to investigate the prices of new cars, rails and sleepers. Meanwhile, arrangements had been made for F. Adams,

No 3 with bogie carriages created from four-wheeled carriage bodies, the ensemble equipped with vacuum brakes. The scales in the left foreground are evidence of the coal trading that led to Dix's departure from Corris.

the Reading Tramway's fitter, to repair the existing carriages, one of the benefits of the railway being part of a larger group. Adams remained at Corris until 27 November, repairing wagons after he had completed the carriages.

The comment about the 'bogie … required for the third engine' is indicative of the loco's position as spare and implies that the other two locos already had bogies, technically pony trucks, fitted to honour the commitment made to the Board of Trade by Kincaid in 1882. With no recorded expenditure on locomotive repairs in 1886, £418 was to be allocated to this heading in 1887. Lambert had found 150 tons of steel Vignoles 41¼lb rail at £3 10s per ton located at Rhymney by 7 October 1886. Fishplates and spikes were required too.

On 9 December 1886 Dix asked the Board of Trade for a meeting to discuss the removal of the mechanical speed governors fitted to the locos in compliance with the 1883 Act. He met Marindin and explained that the devices were regularly breaking and were not required on similar undertakings; Marindin cited the Festiniog Railway and the North Wales Narrow Gauge Railways when he reported on the request. Dix got the approval he sought, providing train speeds did not exceed 12mph, on 20 October.

By February 1887 work on improving the Aberllefenni extension was within a week of completion although the track had not been relaid. Dix suggested making an informal approach to Marindin to ensure that there were no difficulties meeting the Board of Trade's requirements. At the 10 March board meeting the estimate for completion looked a little optimistic. Widening Abercorris cutting, just beyond Corris station, would take two weeks more. Retaining walls at Garneddwen, 100 yards x 3 yards, and Caecoch, 50 yards x 4 yards, also remained outstanding. Dix wanted to employ an additional twelve men to have the line ready to be opened

No 3 equipped with its trailing pony truck and vacuum brakes at Aberllefenni. The large cut-out in the back sheets of the Corris locos were to aid the fireman managing the fire. The smaller cut-out in the blanking plate seen here permitted the vacuum brake pipe to be connected between the locomotive and carriages when hauling trains uphill. (G.H.W. Clifford)

by 1 July. The directors approved five men. Dix arranged for the supply of 6,000 half-round sleepers, 1s 3d, and 2,000 rectangular sleepers, 1s 5d, to be paid for in seven instalments at three-month intervals. Before the directors' meeting on 24 March Lambert had sanctioned the employment of the twelve men Dix had requested.

Half the distance had been relaid, Dix reported on 31 May. The retaining walls at Fronwen cutting, below Garneddwen, were nearly finished. Several adjoining landowners or lessees had been demanding additional level crossings, the land having been subdivided since the line had been built; Dix was to make the best terms possible. Where the line crossed public roads at Corris and Garneddwen, keeper's lodges were required. Dix had rented a cottage at Garneddwen, £5 10s annually inclusive of rates and taxes, and had agreed to buy a plot of land at Corris, £5, for this purpose.

Two weeks later the relaying was within half a mile of Aberllefenni. The line would not be ready until sometime in July. Level crossing gates would cost 15s each, the crossings complete £3. By mid-July the relaying was nearly complete and 'the station was also well advanced'. Hot weather and a water shortage had caused the delay. Both station and relaying were complete by July 27. The level crossings and associated signalling were on the verge of completion and the fencing would take another week. A survey would be carried out to gather the data required by the Board of Trade in anticipation that the inspection would take place during the first week of August.

In the event, it was 9 August 1887 before secretary John W. Alison requested an inspection. Appointed to the task on 16 August, Major General C.S. Hutchinson submitted his report on 31 August. The extension was 1½ miles long, the steepest gradient was 1 in 59, and the sharpest curve had a radius of 5 chains. The only works were three overbridges of 8½ft span, constructed with stone abutments and slab tops, and a river bridge of 12½ft span constructed with stone abutments and stone arch top and local stone retaining walls. Except for some slight settlement in one of the abutments of the river bridge these works appear to have been substantially built and to be standing well. There were two public road crossings, provided with proper gates. One of these appeared to be authorised, he wrote, but at the other, at 5 miles 4 chains, of a side street in Corris, the road should have been diverted and a bridge built.

This crossing had existed since the line had opened, nearly thirty years, however, and no objection had been made to it. Houses had been built around it, it would be costly and difficult to divert the road and build a bridge. By Section 2 of the Act of 1883 the Board of Trade could approve the non-compliance with the plans and he recommended this approach, provided all trains approaching the level crossing from Aberllefenni were required to stop dead before passing over it. If the Act was not considered to give this power, then the company must undertake to get the crossing authorised. The points of two sidings were locked with the train staff and at Corris and Aberllefenni there were signals interlocked with the points.

The requirements were: at Corris, the normal position of the upper points should be for the siding, both sidings should have interlocked catch points; at Aberllefenni a starting signal interlocked with the facing points and trap points above the station were needed; a disc and lamp iron were required for the level crossing gates at 5m 54ch.

At the Board of Trade there was some doubt that the 1883 Act could be used to approve the level crossing, the relevant clause being concerned with curvature, but eventually common sense prevailed: 'the railway is of little importance … there is at present small traffic …', and approval was given on 7 September 1887. The *Cambrian News* reported that the inspection had been made on 24 August and that services had started the next day.

Aberllefenni station was erected on a sliver of land outside the hamlet of that name. So little land was available that the run-round loop had to be located separately, on the Corris side of the station. There was no fuss made when it was opened to passengers in 1887, and there are no known photographs recording the event. This photograph, showing the station's basic facilities, was taken on 19 April 1948, towards the end of the railway's life. The Methodist chapel is beyond it and the dressing shed tips to its right, on the far side of the road. (J.I.C. Boyd)

Views of Aberllefenni showing the station's position in relation to the habitation and the quarry are uncommon. The station is at the lower left of this 1898 view, with a rake of five wagons standing between the gate and the junction of the quarry lines. The Aberllefenni branch passed in front of the row of cottages and then under the Ratgoed branch, while the latter passed behind the cottages before crossing the former, leaving the picture on the centre right. (J. Valentine)

This view of No 2 was taken at the Aberllefenni loop in 1900. Built as bogie vehicles, there are some detail differences around the entrances of the carriages.

Another view of No 2 at Aberllefenni in 1900. The vacuum pipe is visible through the back-sheet opening. The gate separating the passenger railway from the mineral line can be seen just beyond the end of the train.

GARNEDDWEN. 19321

The crossing hut at Garneddwen. Dix seems to have undertaken upgrading the line between Corris and Aberllefenni without reference to George Owen, the engineer. (Donald George)

It should be noted that the line thus approved did not extend to the terminus of the Parliamentary line, nearly half a mile beyond Aberllefenni station. Site restrictions meant that the locomotive run-round loop was outside the station too. The other, authorised, level crossing mentioned by Hutchinson was at Garneddwen, three-quarters of a mile from Corris. Trains stopped there until the 1920s, although it is likely that the Board of Trade was unaware of this.

With £1,556 18s 1d spent against an estimate of £1,500, Imperial wrote the expenditure down against revenue over three years and did not add it to the 'additional expenditure' fund. In 1889 it reported that it had written off, 'a further sum of £250 on account of the Corris Railway (Aberllefenny) Reconstruction.' On 15 September 1887, the directors instructed Alison, 'to convey to Mr Dix the expression of the directors' satisfaction at the way in which he had carried out the reconstruction works.' On 29 November he reported that the extension had earned £57 16s 5d from carrying 3,719 passengers.

The level crossing at Pantperthog, 300 yards below Llwyngwern station, brought the railway into dispute with the highway surveyor for Pennal district from 1 March 1887. He complained that the railway did not keep a lodge, contrary to the Railway Clauses Act 1863 Section 6, and failed to keep a proper person to superintend the crossing. The case was heard at Towyn on 30 September. The surveyor did not expect a gothic cottage, he said, and some provision had been made, but not on the spot as required by the Act. Gate keys were kept at the pandy, a mill cottage about ten yards away, and the noise of the river meant that users had difficulty making themselves heard, leading to delay before they were brought. Dix had replaced small gates by stiles, which did not suit everyone.

The railway's solicitor argued that the pandy was close enough to act as a lodge and the person in charge was a suitable person. Complaints had only been made recently, and were confined to the surveyor and his family. The crossing had only been used eight times in the last month, mostly by people who had used it out of curiosity.

Dix explained that there were four crossings within a mile of this one. Pennal residents wanted a woman who lived in a cottage on the other side of the turnpike appointed to look after it.

After 2½ hours the magistrates had had enough and declared that there had not been sufficient evidence to compel the company to do more than it had done. Considering the evidence as to traffic, the pandy met the requirements of the Act. They did, however, think that Dix should replace the stiles with wicket gates. The directors told him to find a solution that avoided the risk of a penalty in the future.

The crossing was on a minor road between the turnpike and the river, which had a gradient of 1 in 2½. A dispute that had stopped vehicles crossing the river at Llwyngwern had increased its use but it seems that normally using it with a cart was something that residents did in response to a dare. A footpath takes its route. The remains of the pandy are hidden by overgrowth.

After less than five years in service, although it was nearly ten years old, consideration was given to improving the passenger stock, a process that led to the introduction of bogie carriages. In October 1887 Dix started a dialogue with the Falcon Engine & Car Works, successors to Hughes, over the supply of new underframes for the carriages. His opinion that bogie cars would be unsuitable proved to be unfounded.

By 3 November Falcon had quoted £145 each for two vehicles and the next day G.F. Milnes of Birkenhead quoted £110 each for two 12-seat cars 'of tramway type'. Later in the month Milnes quoted £180 for a 24-seat bogie car while Falcon had quoted £210 for a 30-seat car. Asked to quote for a 24-seat vehicle, the Falcon price was £190. Comparing the specifications, Dix thought the Falcon vehicle more suitable and in December 1887 the directors agreed to place an order.

Falcon visited Corris to check the measurements and in February 1888

The ruins of the pandy at Pantperthog that was the centre of the level crossing dispute in 1887. No doubt the lack of mains utilities deters the site's development. The railway trackbed is to the left of the picture.

produced a design that did away with the balconies and which had a single entrance in the centre, offering to supply a 30-seat vehicle for £205 or a 24-seat vehicle for £195. The directors chose the cheaper option. In May 1888 Dix learned that Falcon was proposing to employ a combined centre buffer and coupling on the carriage despite his preference for ordinary buffers. Unable to persuade Falcon to supply buffers without charge, he decided to fit them himself for £2 or £2 10s.

A different approach was considered in June 1888, when Falcon offered to supply an iron frame with bogies on which two four-wheeled car bodies could be mounted. The cost of painting and other work would bring the price to £80. The directors wanted to know the price with a timber frame.

The bogie carriage was delivered on 18 August 1888, when Dix reported that

it ran very satisfactorily. A month later he added that passengers preferred it to the 'ordinary' 1st class carriages; the ride in a 3rd class bogie carriage would have been much better than that in a 1st class four-wheeler.

The big increase in the number of passengers carried in 1888, from 46,586 to 54,178, resulted in the carriage fleet continuing to receive attention. In October, Falcon offered another bogie carriage, with buffers, for £195, £203 if fitted as 1st class or £390 for two ordered together. Approval was given to order one carriage 'similar to the last' on 18 October, paying one-third down and the remainder in six instalments over eighteen months. For conversions, Dix proposed ordering two iron underframes but received approval to order one.

When the directors met on 1 November 1888 Dix proposed that the new carriage

A train with two four-wheeled carriages and the first bogie vehicle just outside Corris station, 1888-93. Ivy hanging from the railway bridge now conceals both bridges from this viewpoint. (Martin Fuller Collection)

be fitted as 1st class, enabling 'the present 1st class' to be made into 3rd class. A compromise was reached, to make it a composite carriage. In August Dix had been instructed to have the existing carriages painted at a cost not to exceed £2 10s each. On 19 October, he had reported that the painting had not been started and that he, 'had had to discard one of the carriages as being not worth repairing.'

The conversion was delivered by 19 March 1889 'and was a decided success' reported Dix. Hearing this on 4 April, the directors resolved not to order 'a second' new carriage 'at present' and that, 'two more of the old carriages should be mounted on a bogie frame.'

Having received a quotation of £113 8s 2d for this conversion Dix wrote to the directors on 3 July, questioning 'the advisability of converting any more as the cost was so great'. A decision was deferred until the directors had visited.

A few months later Dix had changed his mind, asking for another conversion on 12 December but, once again, a decision was deferred.

An article in *The Railway Engineer* published in March 1890 described a new 3rd class bogie carriage, saying that it was designed to carry 24 passengers inside and 2 on the platform. The frames were of oak, the side and corner pillars of English ash. The floor was red deal, one-inch thick, with longitudinal white deal wear strips nailed to it. American elm or English ash was used for the roof. The doors had teak panels and mahogany frames. Mohair blinds were mounted curtain-form on polished brass rods. Wrought iron bogies had each wheel braked, operated by a hand wheel. Dix was credited with its design, and that of the previous bogie stock.

On the railway, a wagon loaded with Abercwmeiddau slate had run away and

Seen c1890, No 1 is ready to leave Machynlleth with a mixed train. A weakness of Dix's bogie carriage design was inadequate ventilation; only one window at each end could be opened. The roof mounted ventilators fitted to the first carriage appear to be an attempt to address the issue. The original Machynlleth station building seems to have done duty as a warehouse and an office, with primitive sanitary facilities causing complaints in 1903. (John Thomas)

Corris c1890. The train would not leave until the photographer had finished. The bogie carriages contrast one that incorporated bodies from the four-wheeled stock (left) and one bought new. (John Thomas)

overturned in December 1887; £3 10s compensation was paid without comment.

Gourley must have used his influence as a director of Sunderland Tramways in June 1888 when a lame horse was sold and two more were required for the 'Talyllyn waggonette'. At a cost of £40 Mr Morrison from Sunderland delivered them in July. How they coped with being spoken to in Welsh was not recorded. They were sold, without comment, for £27 15s in October. Inability to obtain suitable animals in the locality was probably the reason for going to Sunderland, and was the explanation given in June 1889 when Dix was given permission to obtain horses from Ireland – two were purchased for £62 9s including expenses. In October Dix arranged for them

to be wintered at a farm near Machynlleth until 25 March 1890 for £5 inclusive. They were put out to graze, given shelter and hay during inclement weather and visited at least once a week.

Locomotive facilities at Machynlleth were enhanced in June 1888 when Dix had a tube well sunk there to obtain a water supply for them. A galvanised iron tank cost £4 10s. At Maespoeth loco shed the pipes had corroded through by July 1889; their replacements cost £17 10s.

Little detail about the company's administration appears in the minutes but in July 1888 the secretary reported that he had complained to the bank about its charges. The bank agreed to reduce them by half, to ⅛%. Dix's application for an increase in salary made at the same time was deferred until Lambert and Gourley could visit; they agreed to pay him £200 annually from 1 July.

Tipping of waste from Cymerau threatened the stability of the Ratgoed tramway in August 1888. Large boulders had fallen into the stream and diverted it onto the railway formation. Dix's protestations to the quarry manager were ignored but the quarry's underground manager promised remedial action, clearing the stream during October.

Dix reported three incidents with passengers or would-be passengers in November 1888. On 30 October Reverend O.F. Williams, the curate in charge at Corris, jumped into a wagon attached to the 12.15 to Machynlleth at Maespoeth; Dix recommended that consideration of the matter await a further report. He had also summoned two men for riding in 1st class accommodation with 3rd class tickets. Magistrates had dismissed the case but the men would have to pay costs, £2 8s 6d, to the company. On another occasion, three 'persons' connected with the Dulas Slate Company had stopped a train they wanted to travel on by holding up a red handkerchief. This, wrote Dix, being an offence punishable by up to two years imprisonment, he had accepted an offer of £4 4s being donated to the Railway Benevolent Institute and £1 1s to the company to cover its legal expenses.

The *Aberystwyth Times* described the half-day excursion from Aberystwyth to Corris on 25 October 1888 as the first organised visit to the slate-producing area. The reduced-fare tickets on offer attracted eighty-one participants but the paper thought there would have been more if the weather had not been dull and cloudy. Its contributor was amused by the sight of a pony cart seen heading in the same direction as the narrow-gauge train left Machynlleth, which arrived at Corris just as the excursionists left the station. The paper acknowledged Dix's contribution to the event, which included trips to Braich Goch quarry and Talyllyn and a meal.

It seems, though, that normally little thought was given to encouraging Aberystwyth visitors to visit Corris. In July 1889 the *Aberystwith Observer* told how those leaving the seaside town by the 10.00am train found that there was no connection at Machynlleth, but that there had been one for the 9.00am departure, and in August 1891 Herbert Wix, a visitor, complained to the paper that he had picked up a leaflet offering 'summer fares' valid on the 9.00am and 12.15pm departures but when he tried to book for the 9.00am he was told the special fares were only valid on the 7.40am and 12.15pm trains. Showing the booking clerk the leaflet, he was told it was a Corris Railway publication, not the Cambrian Railways.

The Dulas Slate Company was in financial difficulties by January 1889, owing £16 13s 9d for carriage. Dix seized two loads of goods as a lien for the debt; when he accepted ten shillings in the pound a year later no mention was made of the goods seized. After Abercorris quarry changed hands, was reconstructed, and asked for a credit account in 1890, the directors checked the status of the proprietors. The slate trade was showing signs of picking up, reported Dix, saying that Braich Goch had started working full time.

An eisteddfod held in Corris on 10 June 1889, Whit Monday, was Dix's initiative. The event attracted a large audience, 1,166 passengers were carried and £18 0s 10d taken in fares. In contrast, in August 1889 Dix reported that slate traffic was depressed because a strike in the Ffestiniog quarries had resulted in stocks there being sold off.

The minutes contain regular reports about the other employees. Lewis Lewis, a gatekeeper, had worked for the railway for twenty years in 1889. He was 77 years old and unable to perform his duties, reported Dix, asking if a small pension could be granted. The directors agreed to pay 2s 6d per week for a year.

Richard Davies, Llwyngwern station master, appeared in court in

December 1889. The report is quoted in full: 'This man has been charged by Colonel Morris's keeper with poaching while looking after some wood which he had bought from Mr Gillart's woodman. He had been summoned and fined 6d with costs. The manager had information that both the charge and the magistrate's decision were unjust. Colonel Morris wished that the man should be discharged. The manager, however, stated that Davies had been a good servant to the company and had been unjustly charged: Resolved that Davies be retained in the service.' The incident had occurred on 8 November and Davies was fined £1.

How many platelayers the railway normally employed is not known. In March 1890 Dix reported that they had applied for a pay rise of 1s per week and to be allowed to finish at 1pm on Saturdays. Dix's proposal to give them the same pay and conditions as Cambrian platelayers was approved.

The directors had a fatality to consider when they had met on 3 October 1889. A child, Laura Pugh Davies, had strayed onto the Braich Goch branch on 18 September and had been run down by two wagons 'rounding a curve'. Returning a verdict of accidental death, the coroner's jury recommended the branch be fenced off and the men in charge of wagons be enjoined to use great caution in descending the inclines; presumably they meant steep gradients. The Board of Trade wanted to know if the recommendations would be acted upon. Dix arranged to fence the 'Braich curve'.

Compliance with the 1889 Regulation of Railways Act was considered on 31 October 1889. Dix had arranged for tickets to be printed bearing the fares and considered it probable that the Board of Trade would not require the company to adopt continuous brakes. Dix was wrong in his assumption, so started a correspondence that went on intermittently for five years.

'Section 1(a) (the block system) does not apply to us,' wrote Dix on 21 December, 'as we work with only one engine in steam or two coupled together. Section 1(b) (interlocking of points and signals) does not apply because our passenger lines were passed in 1883 and 1887 and the existing requirements complied with. Section 1(c) (continuous brakes) – none of our passenger stock is provided with continuous brakes but all our vans and carriages are fitted with hand brakes applying to all wheels and … enable our trains to be stopped … in the length of the train. As our line is a narrow gauge of 2ft 3in gauge I beg to ask that we may be exempted from having to adopt a continuous automatic brake.' Regarding mixed trains, he explained that all trains were mixed and 90% of wagons were private owner vehicles. Making the usual excuses about the railway's narrow gauge and low speed he asked for it to be exempted from the requirements.

A clipping from the *Oswestry & Border Counties Advertiser* of 6 November reporting the railway's success at carrying over 30,000 passengers during the year was carefully filed in the Board of Trade file; perhaps someone there thought that it showed the railway was busier than it represented itself. There appeared to be no hurry, for it was not until 4 March 1890 that Dix's appeal was repeated by the secretary. The draft order was prepared the next day, allowing no exception for continuous brakes and a six-month extension of time to fit them. Mixed trains 'might be allowed on the same condition as on the Talyllyn Railway'. Alison wrote again on 20 November, asking that 'as the company's passenger stock is in course of being remodelled and reconstructed I am directed to ask that the period for applying continuous brakes may be extended to three years from the date of the order' and for the railway to be allowed to run three mixed trains daily between Machynlleth and Aberllefenni. The order was made the same day, allowing the three years without demur. The question of the mixed trains would be considered in due course.

Reporting the order's obligations to the directors' meeting on 11 December 1890,

Dix recommended, 'the engine about to be repaired should be fitted with the automatic vacuum brake and that the six remaining old carriages be fitted on three new bogie frames at the rate of one new frame per year to be fitted with the brake apparatus; the cost of the brake being £50 per engine, £15 per carriage, £20 for the guard's van. He recommended the vacuum automatic brake be adopted.' The directors adopted Dix's proposals, but in January 1892, when they agreed to his request to order two sets of brakes for carriages, costing £12 each, he was asked to report on the relative qualities of the vacuum brake and the Westinghouse brake. Both complied with Board of Trade requirements, he reported, 30,339 vehicles were fitted with vacuum brakes and 15,164 with Westinghouse. The £278 spent on rolling stock repairs in 1892, much higher than in either the preceding or following years, probably included brake equipment.

The decision to put the third locomotive into traffic had followed an incident on 25 September 1890, when a tube burst on the loco hauling the 6.40am train from Machynlleth, delaying traffic by two hours. Identified as 'engine No 2', the directors accepted a tender of £105

15s for its repair 'in accordance with specification' on 8 January 1891. It was sent to Loughborough, the railway paying for its carriage. On 10 March Dix reported that repairs were in progress and that he would travel to Loughborough to observe its steam test. Locomotive repairs cost £655 in 1891, increased from £340 the year before, and £502 in 1892.

Braich Goch's 'right of access' to the railway's main line was an unexpected victim of the 1890 order. Dix wrote to the directors on 3 December 1890, saying that having escaped an obligation to adopt the block system it was 'most desirable that the Braich Goch haulage should be performed by the company'. Braich Goch responded by asking if the railway would purchase its wagons and provide them for its future use and if the railway would enter into an agreement to allow Braich Goch to be restored to its existing position. Dix advised against such an agreement, saying that Braich Goch had no statutory right to perform its own haulage. He was told to ask Braich Goch to justify its position.

Perhaps before he had done so, Dix informed the directors that although the 1858 Act did not directly convey any rights on Braich Goch it did incorporate the 1845

Seen at Machynlleth soon after it had been rebuilt and equipped with vacuum brakes in 1898, No 2 was photographed with a train of five bogie carriages and a van.

Railway Clauses Consolidation Act and quoted from clause No 92: 'upon payment of the tolls from time to time demandable all companies and persons shall be entitled to use the railway, with *engines* and carriages properly constructed.' The company had, however, obtained a legal opinion in 1887 to the effect that clause No 9 of the 1880 Act gave the company the, 'right to prevent the Braich Goch Company from carrying their slates over any of the portion of the line open for passenger traffic.' The relevant section reads: 'In the event of the company conveying passengers on the railways … by means of steam or locomotive power, the company shall convey … upon the terms and conditions contained in the act of 1858, the articles, matters, and things set forth in that act: provided always, that the company shall not be required to find carriages or wagons for the conveyance of such articles, matters, and things.'

Meeting on 5 February 1891, the directors resolved to give Braich Goch notice that after 30 June its use of the main line would cease and that the railway would carry its traffic at the statutory rates. The letter was to be drafted for approval at the next meeting. Before that occasion, following an intervention by Dix, they had reverted to their previous position and he had told Braich Goch that the railway did not want to buy the wagons or enter into an agreement. When no reply had been received by 2 April 1891 it was decided to serve notice that Braich Goch should discontinue its main line haulage from 29 June.

Details of the subsequent correspondence between the parties was not recorded in the minutes until 25 June 1891, when the secretary reported that he had visited Braich Goch on 5 June and had reached agreement that the railway would undertake the quarry's haulage at a rate of 2s per ton from 1 July, bringing forty-two years of private haulage between Corris and Machynlleth to an end.

Earlier, on 22 January 1891 Dix had raised the question of the private owner wagons in general, saying that the wheels of most of them were in 'a very bad state of repair' and recommending the quarries be served with a formal notice requiring the wagons to comply with defined standards from 1 July. The directors agreed that a notice should be drafted by the solicitor.

The next time the railway heard from the Board of Trade was when it received a letter dated 20 December 1893 which appeared to ask, the file copy has not survived, the railway's position regarding the 1889 Act. Writing from Bristol on 19 January 1894, secretary Samuel White repeated the points made by his predecessor, adding that continuous brakes had been fitted to all the rolling stock except for two carriages that had been withdrawn for it to be fitted and that, 'it was not the practice of this railway to take advantage of the modification which permits one unbraked vehicle at the tail of the train.'

Reviewing White's letter, the Board of Trade realised that the undertaking concerning the method of working should have been amended to say that the engine should carry a staff. 'The remainder of the reply is satisfactory.' The amended undertaking was given on 5 February 1894. Capital expenditure during 1893 was £155, for vacuum brakes, a charabanc, a horse and additional stabling.

At Aberllefenni, construction of a siding to serve a new works for Ashton, Green, Matthews & Company had been started in October 1889. Located at 6 miles 6.18 chains, it replaced an earlier siding at 6 miles 11.90 chains. The railway did the work at a cost of £91 paid for by the company. The Board of Trade was informed on 4 February 1890, when Dix explained that a trap point had been put in one chain from the points and that the siding was 'now level for 1.50 chains and then [on] a falling gradient of 1 in 25 from the main line'.

Railway inspector Colonel F.H. Rich submitted his report from Dublin on 7 August 1890. Because of the gradient the railway undertook only to insert and remove wagons when the engine was at the south end of the train. Subject to the point rods being secured by steel cotters or a nut and split pin, instead of split pins only, and the stock rail kept to gauge with a tie bar he recommended the works be approved. The alterations were carried out by 19 August. On the 1901 Ordnance Survey map the site was called Matthew's Mill.

The Talyllyn and posting traffic did well in 1889, receipts for the year reaching £110 10s 6d compared with £57 15s 3d, but when Dix suggested buying a 10-seat waggonette for the traffic the directors asked for details of the service's running costs. Producing a figure of £48, Dix received approval to purchase the vehicle. When it was not delivered until September 1890 he negotiated a reduction in price to £20. In June 1891 Dix bought the Braich Goch Inn's waggonette, which he had been in the habit of borrowing at peak times, for £6.

The carriages came back on the railway's agenda at the end of 1889 when Dix's proposal to convert two more of the four-wheelers into a bogie carriage was rebuffed by the directors. However, when he returned to the subject in January 1890 he was successful. On this occasion Brush Electrical Engineering, successors to Hughes and Falcon, had offered to do the conversion, complete with fittings and painting for £87 19s including transport. Dix's estimate of an additional expenditure of £30 for unspecified alterations and repairs, the same job was implied, was also accepted.

In September 1890 it was the wagons' turn to make an appearance in the minutes. Several wagon wheels having become worn out, Dix had ordered six wheelsets from Hadfield of Sheffield at £7 19s 6d per set. He had obtained prices from other suppliers but Hadfield's had proved the most satisfactory in the past, which may be taken to mean that they were not the cheapest. The railway had a need for trucks to carry timber, reported Dix, proposing to build two for £10 each.

The encouragement of summer visitors to Corris was facilitated by an arrangement Dix made with the Cambrian Railways in February 1890 for through tickets to be sold at Aberystwyth, Borth, Aberdyfi, Towyn, Barmouth and Dolgelley. On

12 April 1890, the *Aberystwyth Observer* used the railway as an exemplar of how railways should perform. In its report on the Manchester & Milford Railway, which had seen a decrease in receipts of £123, it commented that this seemed strange when the Cambrian Railways and other lines had reported increases and felt that more could be done to increase tourist traffic. 'Last summer 30,000 tourists travelled over the little Corris Railway, and the managers of the M&M might well take a hint from the management of the Corris line.'

After buying horses from Sunderland and Ireland, in May 1890 Dix proposed buying one from Aberystwyth fair, a little closer to home. One of the horses had gone lame so another was needed for the Talyllyn traffic. He paid £30 for a bay mare. He was unable to sell the Irish horses in November 1890 so put them out to grass near Borth for 10s each per month, telling the directors that he expected to achieve the purchase price when he sold them in the spring. The bay was sold for £30 in June 1891. At the same time, he told the directors that he would need to buy two horses for the summer traffic. In October, he sold two at Machynlleth fair, one bought in 1889 for £26 sold for £15 and one bought in 1890 for £31 sold for £26.

Abercwmeiddau was in trouble again in April 1890, owing £47 8s 8d, although £23 had been paid on account. Dix told the quarry that without regular monthly payments the railway would cease to give credit. By May the quarry had paid up to March and Dix insisted on monthly payments.

Apart from the initial problems with retaining walls following the line's reconstruction for steam locomotives, its infrastructure was rarely mentioned. By September 1890 though, the timber beams of a bridge at Aberllefenni had become unsafe for traffic. They could be repaired for £25 said Dix, telling the directors that replacing the timber with iron would be considerably more expensive.

William Williams travelled from Llwyngwern to Machynlleth on 23 October 1890 and jumped off the train as it

CORRIS RAILWAY TRAIN CROSSING THE DOVEY. 18599

In 1892/3 a photographer had a train stopped on the Dyfi bridge for him to photograph. The driver is leaning on the fence, in front of the smokebox, waiting for the picture to be taken. (J. Valentine)

approached the station to avoid the fare. This was a double offence and the directors supported Dix's recommendation to prosecute. When Williams offered to pay £1 and agreed to notices being distributed describing his offences the summons was withdrawn.

Deterioration in the main line sleepers was reported by Dix in March 1891, barely three years after their installation had been completed. He proposed a programme of replacing 2,000 annually, paying 1s 6d for the first 2,000. As an experiment he had pickled 904 sleepers in carbolineum avenarius, a tar oil preservative, at a cost of 3d each and was satisfied with the results. The Ratgoed branch was in poor condition and required 2,000 sleepers which could be obtained for 11d each. The main line purchase was approved. Dix was to make enquiries about the suitability of using 9ft red Baltic sleepers cut in half. The directors were not fully convinced by the treated sleeper he sent to London for them to inspect but obviously saw the benefit of treating the timber, resolving to obtain tenders for creosoted sleepers.

Six tenders for red Baltic sleepers had been received by 30 April 1891 with prices ranging from 11d to 1s 3¾d untreated

and 1s 2½d to 1s 7¼d treated delivered to Machynlleth. 2,000 untreated sleepers were ordered from E.A. Jones of Wrexham at 11d each, A.J. Jones of Aberdyfi undertaking to creosote them for 3½d each. 250 were to be treated with carbolineum. The Ratgoed sleepers were delivered by July 1891.

On 14 September 1891 Dix reported the discovery of a leak in the boiler on 'engine No 3', several of the pipes in the smokebox required renewing. The work was estimated to cost £10.

The Dyfi bridge required attention, Dix wrote on 4 November 1891, the ends of eight longitudinal beams were rotten. Replacements cost £10 and were installed on 6 November; the train service ran to Fridd Gate while the work was being carried out.

Dix was rebuked after telling the directors that he had accepted an offer from Ferndale Collieries to supply steam coal during 1892 for £1 3s 3d per ton. He was told 'in future to obtain the sanction of the board before making contracts'. At the next meeting, 14 January 1892, his report that the previous price had been £1 4s 6d was accepted without comment.

When the line was blocked by snow for several days in January 1892, Dix's response to quarry owners who complained about delays to services was approved by the directors.

In 1892 the company came under pressure from the Cambrian Railways to join the Railway Clearing House to benefit from revenue sharing on through traffic with particular reference to the Post Office (Parcels) Act of 1882. The sharing arrangement for parcels was being reviewed and the Cambrian claimed that the company would benefit by £32 per year. The secretary was deputed to attend a conference of general managers dealing with the issue and Dix proposed registering with the GPO to become a party to the Act. The directors, however, resolved to enquire if the company might be able to make special terms with the GPO if it remained independent. The returns show that the railway had been paid for carrying mails since 1883 and had been paid £50 annually since 1888. On learning that there would be no benefit in remaining independent, on 26 February 1892 the directors resolved to register.

A long-standing dispute over charges for using the bridge owned by the Dulas Slate Company at Esgairgeiliog that was crossed by the Era slate quarry branch was revived in March 1892. The minute explained that the railway had originally been allowed free use in exchange for providing the siding to the slate enamel works. When the property changed hands in 1885 a wayleave was demanded, originally £5 but settled at £1 in 1886. Despite agreeing to it the company appears not to have paid it. Now the owner was demanding £10 and had blocked the bridge. Before responding, the directors decided to investigate the likely effect on traffic at the station; Dix recommended removing the point.

Instructed to establish whether, if the company paid £6 to cover the previous six years, it could have free use of the bridge for all traffic on 24 March 1892, Dix reported that the owner claimed to have been in possession since 1884 and wanted £10 for eight years' use and to be informed of the station's traffic with a view to regulating charges in future. The directors decided to take no further action.

There was an unintended consequence to this affair for the bridge's owner, who charged Esgairgeiliog villagers a toll for using it. Dix sold them some timber so they could build a footbridge across the river and avoid it. In June 1894 a changed board was to instruct Dix to agree to the owner's terms for using the bridge.

Dix continued the carriage conversion programme, no doubt in accordance with the resolution of December 1890. However, when he submitted a report in respect of a vehicle that had been completed in March on 11 April 1892 he was again rebuked for acting without the directors' approval.

The Cambrian Railways threatened Dix's equanimity over the Talyllyn traffic when he discovered that the larger company had advertised a coach to run from Towyn to the lake from 1 June 1892 and also wanted to run a service from Machynlleth to the lake, the latter in direct competition with the railway's well-established service. In response, Dix obtained Ward's approval to bring his service forward to start on 1 June as well. The Cambrian's traffic manager appeared to think that there was an agreement that the Corris service would not start until 1 July and responded by limiting the through tickets from coastal stations to one train a day. Dix was instructed to meet the Cambrian and restore good relations. On 16 June, 'The secretary was instructed to intimate to the manager that the board are dissatisfied at hearing no further report from him as to this matter [arrangement with Cambrian Railways] and to desire that a general report be furnished for the information of every board meeting.'

By the time the board met on 30 June 1892 Dix could report that he had established a rapport with the Cambrian, through ticketing had been restored in full and a circular tour from the coastal stations via Corris and Towyn had been arranged. If there was any benefit for the company from the last it was not stated. June receipts for the Talyllyn coach had been £16 19s 9d. Two more horses might be required. One was sold for 15s in October. It had been used since 1885 but had developed a cracked heel. Two spare horses were being wintered for £5. Dix was instructed to rotate the horses in use.

Never one to miss an opportunity to publicise the railway, on 15 September 1892 Dix and a group of Corris quarrymen visited Barmouth to wait upon the prime minister, W.E. Gladstone, who was passing through the town on his way home after staying with his friend Sir Edward Watkin at Beddgelert. Dix and the quarrymen presented Gladstone with an album of photographs, hoping that the charms of Talyllyn and Corris as illustrated therein would encourage him to visit. They were in competition with a team from Aberystwyth but neither were successful.

Unchanged since 1885, the company's board saw several changes in 1891/2. Chairman A.J. Lambert attended for the last time on 14 May 1891 and died on 22 September, aged 52. William Ward signed the minutes 'chairman pro tem' until 23 July, also the date of a general meeting, after which he signed as chairman. George White of Bristol was elected a director on 12 November 1891 and Ward was formally elected chairman on 26 November.

At the time of his death the *South Wales Daily News* recorded Lambert's interests in the Swansea Improvements & Tramways Company, the Anglo-Argentine Tramway Company, the Bordeaux Tramway & Omnibus Company and the Hull Street Tramway Company as well as Imperial Tramways.

White had been secretary of the Bristol Tramways & Carriage Company since 1875 and was now the largest shareholder in Imperial. The changes he wrought there were carried through to the Corris Railway.

Hugh Charles Godfray, not Godfrey, a solicitor, became an additional director in 1892, attending his first board meeting on 25 February although his election was not formally recorded. A more significant change occurred on 11 August when White and Godfray proposed that James Clifton Robinson be elected managing director of the company, a move that was followed

by Ward's resignation as a director and White's election as chairman.

Robinson had a long career in tramways, working for George Francis Train on the first British tramway in Birkenhead in his youth. His obituary (*The Times* 8 November 1910) records that from 1875 to 1882 he had run Bristol Tramways for the railway's erstwhile engineer Joseph Kincaid. In 1892 he had returned from a two-year assignment for the American Street Railway Association to become Imperial Tramways' managing director.

Gourley resigned on 19 September 1892. Knighted in 1895, he died on 15 April 1902 and is remembered by a prominent memorial erected in Sunderland's Mere Knolls cemetery. Godfray was appointed the company's solicitor on 27 October 1892. Secretary Alison resigned on 23 November, 'as arranged with the directors of the owning company, the Imperial Tramways Company.' The meeting adjourned to Godfray's office where it was resolved to transfer the registered office to Clare Street House in Bristol and to appoint Samuel White, George White's brother, as secretary.

Consequences of the new order were that Dix lost his contact with the directors, dealing with Robinson alone, board meetings became less frequent and entries in the minutes were restricted to the approval of cheques and proposed dividends and such comments as, 'Various traffic details were considered and settled.' If they continued, the payments to Imperial Tramways were no longer recorded. Since 1885 £2,950 had been paid; this money has not been identified in the railway or Imperial accounts. In 1892 the railway's debt to Imperial was £611.

In parallel with these changes, James Fraser, whose involvement with the railway pre-dated 1874, was negotiating to sell it to the Cambrian, reporting on 16 November 1892 that negotiations were continuing. In June 1895 White reported being informed by Fraser that the Cambrian directors had rejected the proposed terms for leasing the railway. Neither the Cambrian officers nor its directors thought it necessary to make any record of the negotiations.

Approaching the completion of ten years of steam and passenger operation and an almost complete change of direction, it is appropriate to review the railway's performance. One thing that stands out is that the dividends were much lower than they had been before 1878: ranging from nothing in 1890 to 5% in 1885, the average was less than 3%. Passenger traffic had grown steadily from less than 50,000 in 1884 and regularly exceeded 55,000 from 1888. Merchandise was static through the decade while slate was roundly 16,000 tons per year, dipping to 13,546 tons in 1891. Costs however were considerably increased, rising from £1,688 in 1884 to £2,847 in 1892, reflecting not only the cost of maintaining the locos and keeping the track fit for passenger trains but also an increase in annual train mileage of nearly 4,000 miles over the period. The three years of posting and Talyllyn coach traffic and revenue available during this period are insufficient to make any generalisations about it.

Meeting in London on 6 April 1893, with Fraser in the chair and Godfray and Robinson present, Samuel White presented George White's and Robinson's report on rolling stock. They had authorised another carriage conversion, the 'alteration of one engine and one guard's van and the fitting of automatic brakes to the whole of the vehicles named …' Dix had been to Loughborough to arrange the, 'extra repairs necessary, the repairs and alterations to the locomotive being completed at Corris, the manager having arranged to supplement his own staff with any assistance necessary to finish off that portion of the work.'

There were to be no further reports about the rolling stock, leaving the stories of the locomotive overhauls and carriage conversions incomplete. 1893 expenditure included £435 on locomotive repairs and £201 on carriage repairs.

Authorisation for Dix to order uniforms, cost about £25, on the same occasion implies that they had not been a feature of operations previously. A uniform button is illustrated on page 178.

An accident caused by 'slippery state of metals and brakes failing to act' occurred on the Tyddynyberth branch in October 1893. The several wagons of Braich Goch slate involved would cost £17 or £18 to repair, Dix reported, adding that 'no injury was caused to any of the brakesmen attending to the wagons', indicative of wagons still being run to Maespoeth by gravity.

Following a complaint from the Board of Trade, on 29 June 1894 Dix was instructed to acquire land for a waiting room at Corris. He had first raised this issue in May 1892, when the company had been given notice to quit the stables, suggesting that a plot of land next to the station be purchased and used to accommodate a waiting room, stable and coach house but the directors had not been interested. On 3 November 1892 Merioneth County Council had passed a resolution calling upon the railway to provide a waiting room, noting that people working up a sweat while running for a train were at risk of catching a chill waiting in the open.

Perhaps Dix had heard of the proposal to lease the railway to the Cambrian but when Robinson had told the directors on 2 August 1894 that he [Dix] had expressed an interest in leasing the line himself their response was quite fierce: 'The secretary was instructed to write to Mr Dix expressing the view of the board that assuming from his application he was under the impression he could work the railway to better advantage, they expected him to exercise all his energies for the company's benefit.'

The directors were probably unaware of his appointment as engineer of the then proposed 3ft gauge railway between Welshpool and Llanfair Caereinion, reported by the *Aberystwith Observer* on 26 April 1890, for which he produced a set of plans; John Francis was one of the line's promoters, or that in September 1891 he had also been one of the candidates selected for interview to replace John Conacher as secretary and general manager of the Cambrian Railways.

The directors were also likely to have been unaware of the patent that Dix had obtained for a device that sounds remarkably like a trip cock, for preventing trains from passing signals at danger, in 1893. *Academie Parisienne des Inventeurs* gave him an award for it and in 1901, around the time that trip cocks were first used on London's underground railways, he sold the patent. Whether the trip cocks complied with it or whether the purchase was to prevent a claim for infringement is not known.

Notwithstanding the rebuke, Dix presented evidence for the company's appeal against its rating assessment on 26 September 1894. In Machynlleth it had been increased from £15 to £40, in Pennal parish, 3½ miles of railway plus the stations at Fridd Gate, Llwyngwern and Esgairgeiliog, advertisement hoardings and a house, from £52 to £215. The assistant overseer explained that this was because when the old assessment had been made the railway did not carry passengers. After an adjournment, the Machynlleth rate was reduced to £30 and the Pennal rate to £125.

Dix also appealed against the reduced Pennal rate in July 1895, saying that it bore no comparison with the Talyllyn Railway's assessment. Although the traffic on the two railways was not comparable, the assessors replied, the Corris rate would be reduced to £113.

A 'slight accident' had occurred on 5 February 1895, reported the *Montgomery County Times*. 'During shunting operations a truck got off the line and was upset, and a carriage was forced on top of it. Being a "light" railway the vehicles were soon got onto the rails again.' The location was not given.

A man and two women appeared at Towyn petty sessions in July 1895, charged with trespass on the railway, using the Dyfi bridge as a short-cut on 16 May, Machynlleth fair day. Appealing for leniency, Dix said that he wanted to stop the practice, not punish the defendants, who were fined 2s 6d each, including costs.

Dix and two horse drivers appeared in the dock at the same court on 27 September 1895, facing two charges of causing horses to be ill-treated, their drivers being charged for driving them while having sores and in an unfit state for working. Dix was fined 30s and 11s costs on each charge, the drivers 10s and 11s costs each.

The death of another horse, run down by a train on 29 June 1895, resulted in an appearance at Machynlleth county court on 19 October, contesting a claim for a mare run down while chasing after its foal. The company denied liability and maintained that the fence was adequate, but other witnesses gave evidence that it was rotten. The jury awarded £40 in damages and the judge awarded costs 'on the high court scale', total £79 8s 2d. The imposition of costs at the higher rate may be taken as a rebuke of the company's conduct of its defence, or even express the judge's opinion that the case was indefensible. Reporting to the board in November, Robinson commented that, 'It seemed a very extraordinary decision … there was no chance of appealing successfully.'

Another claim brought against the company concerned a strip of land between the railway and the river at Pont Ifans. Part of the railway's crossing cottage stood on a section of it but ownership was claimed by Walter Hume Long, an MP from Wiltshire, owner of the Coedwig estate, at the end of 1897. As the cottage is not shown on the 1887 edition of the six-inch Ordnance Survey map but is shown on the 1900 edition, it could be that it had only been built recently. Capital expenditure of £98 6s in 1896 might account for it.

After making an offer that would have inhibited railway operation if executed, Long succeeded with a court action at Dolgellau assizes on 7 July 1899. His employment of a London QC and another MP to argue his cause no doubt contributed to the judgment being made in his favour.

The year 1897 had started with a series of anonymous letters published in

Y Negesydd, a Welsh-language newspaper. The first, from 'Tyst' (Witness), complained about the way staff treated passengers travelling on the Saturday evening train from Corris to Aberllefenni, saying that when it was ready to leave passengers were pushed onto it and he heard one of them comment that they were being packed as if they were rashers of bacon. Several were standing on the platform between the compartments as well, which he thought was forbidden. Adding another carriage to the train would have made things much easier, he thought. Everyone had paid for a ticket, the staff should make sure they got a seat.

'Teithwr' (Traveller) replied two weeks later, saying that the real issue was the behaviour of some of the passengers, he called them cannibals, who would not join the train until the last minute, and then crowded on. The editor published another letter from each of the correspondents,

attacking each other, before closing the 'discussion', but published a letter from 'Dwygiwr' (Dancer) in February. Saying that he had no problem with the railway's officers, he protested that Corris station was unworthy of the name. There was nowhere to wait when it was cold, the horses had better accommodation. He did not have to wait too long for improvement, because on 13 March the Montgomery County Times reported that work on a waiting room had started. What Dix seems to have done, however, was to appropriate a part of the carriage shed for a new booking office, with door and a ticket window accessible from the platform, and converted the previous booking office into the waiting room. An external door previously in the carriage shed wall was replaced by a window.

Only five years since the council and the Board of Trade had raised the issue, waiting passengers must have found it

Railway horses and their groom pose outside the entrance to the coach room on the upper level of the stable block. Now housing the railway's museum, the building was erected in 1896. (MRFS)

quite galling to see building works for the railway's live and dead stock taking priority, with expenditure of £333 on new stables added to the capital account in 1896. Constructed on an irregular sloping site, the new building housed six or seven horses on a lower level, and a parcels office, coach house, harness room and hayloft on the same level as the station.

The introduction of the Light Railways Act in 1896, with its offer of treasury grants and loans to encourage the construction of new railways to develop remote areas, encouraged many rural local authorities to see how they could benefit. On 2 December 1897 Dolgellau's Rural District Council resolved to petition the company to extend to the county town. No reply had been received by 11 January 1898, when the council noted that Talyllyn District Council gave its support to the scheme.

It was February 1899 before Dix met a councillor to discuss the idea, which must be indicative of the urgency attached to it, but when Porthmadog civil engineer Thomas Roberts said that he wanted £21 to produce a rough plan and section, the council accepted a proposition to postpone the matter for another six months, from 31 October 1899, one of the councillors saying, 'Undoubtedly the railway would be a good thing, but the council had neither the means nor the money just yet to assist in bringing it about.'

In Montgomeryshire, there was much discussion about the use of a narrow gauge railway to link Llanfair Caereinion with Welshpool, following the failure of earlier proposals, and on 30 April 1898 the *Montgomery County Times* published a 2,000-word feature explaining the Corris Railway's history and features and how they could be applicable to light railways.

The anonymous author had visited Corris and spoken to Dix.

Key points were: expenditure on rebuilding the railway for locomotives and acquiring and rebuilding carriages and wagons had been from revenue; seven miles of the railway's eleven miles laid with steel rails were locomotive worked, the remainder was horse worked; the railway owned 18 wagons, the quarries about 150; the largest number of passengers carried on one day had been 1,466; the largest number in a week, 3,293; during August-October 1879, the omnibus service had carried 4,632 passengers.

The railway had carried 72,822 passengers in six months, represented by 53,902 single-journey tickets and 18,920 journeys made by school children and workmen using weekly tickets. If this number could be carried in an area with a population of only 4,000, the writer espoused, then more heavily populated areas should be encouraged to obtain light railways, ignoring the Corris area's popularity with tourists that accounted for a large proportion of the single tickets issued. These figures probably relate to a half-year from April to September as they do not match figures in the annual reports. To illustrate the railway's flexibility, when a 'strolling company' or show visited Machynlleth, Dix would offer to run a special train in return for a guarantee of £1 in fares. On the rare occasions that the guarantee was called upon, it seldom amounted to more than 5s, and the promoter recouped the cost from the extra tickets sold.

Finally, statistics were used to show that in terms of the average number of passengers carried per mile, the tiny Corris Railway was more successful than the mighty LNWR:

	Miles worked by engines	No of passengers	Average No of passengers per mile of line	Miles run by passenger trains	Average No of passengers per mile run
Cambrian	256	1,239,016	4,839.9	509,651	2.43
LNWR	2,862	40,109,720	13,980.3	12,221,163	3.28
Corris	6½	41,905	6,445.9	8,647	4.84

On 21 May 1898, the paper published a response from the engineer E.R. Calthrop, saying that the railway's story exemplified the triumph of the narrow-gauge principle over popular prejudice and should encourage Welshpool residents to support their own light railway. He was certain that if the Corris Railway had been standard gauge, built at the average cost of such railways in England, it would have been a financial failure. 'It goes without saying,' he concluded, 'that even a narrow-gauge railway will not give satisfactory results unless the management is in the hands of as competent and able a manager as Mr Dix has proved himself to be.'

Five 'trams' loaded with coal and oil had run away from Maespoeth on 5 February 1898, reported the *Montgomery County Times* a week later. The crossing gates at Llwyngwern and Fridd Gate were smashed before they were stopped by a train loaded with lime at Machynlleth. The paper's claim that the wagons covered five miles in four minutes, average speed 75mph, seems unlikely.

Under the heading 'Miniature Railway', the *Aberystwyth Times*, 28 July 1898,

announced the acquisition of a new locomotive, except that things were not quite as the newspaper thought, for No 2 had 'simply' been rebuilt. There is no reason to doubt the statements that it now possessed a steel boiler with copper firebox and brass tubes, Rowan's patent pistons and automatic vacuum brake. Working at 180lb per square inch instead of 120lb made the loco capable of hauling longer, heavier trains, the paper declared. The boiler was slightly larger than that originally fitted, to increase its capacity. All three locomotives were rebuilt to the same specification.

The addition to stock of two bogie carriages built by the Metropolitan Railway Carriage & Wagon Company during the year went unnoticed, and almost unrecorded. However, Imperial Tramways' report for the first half of the year noted 'further exceptional outlay in permanent way and rolling stock renewals', the year's expenditure on the railway totalling £2,763 12s 10d.

Unchanged from £7,732 2s 2d since 1886, the 'additional expenditure' item

An unusual perspective of a short train in the platform of the original Machynlleth station, seen on 23 September 1891. Part of one of the four-wheeled carriages is just visible on the left of the picture.

Locomotives Nos 2 and 3, seven carriages and a van pause for a photograph on the Dyfi bridge c1909. The train appears to be about half full. (Donald George)

in Imperial's accounts did not appear as a separate item after that company was restructured on 28 September 1898. The 1878 company had been put into liquidation and a new company registered with the same name. Thereafter, the value of Imperial's capital assets and investments was amalgamated. (The holders of £6 shares in the old company received £10 shares in the new one, the difference covered by the increase in the company's capital value.)

Dix's continued prominence in the community is illustrated by a report in the *Aberystwyth Observer*, 22 December 1898. He had arranged a series of weekly lantern slide lectures, temperance events, that had proved very popular. Held in the village school on Saturdays, the audience was entertained by songs and recitations during the interval, when the opportunity was also taken to drink tea or coffee and smoke. In December 1901 he led the committee that welcomed the return of a Boer War hero, Lieutenant Hubert de Burgh Edwards DSO, the vicar's son, to Corris, which included laying out detonators along the railway.

His versatility and usefulness to the company is demonstrated by his appearance in Machynlleth magistrates' court to prosecute a labourer, David Davies, for travelling without a ticket on 5 April 1899. Davies had been seen joining the train at Machynlleth but denied having been on it when asked for his ticket at Fridd Gate. In court he gave various excuses and said that he had intended to pay later. The fare was 1d, explained Dix. Had he, Davies, offered to pay, and not denied travelling, proceedings would not have been taken, but there had been many cases of passengers avoiding paying their fares. The practice was 'obnoxious', declared the magistrates, fining Davies 11s including costs.

Dix also prosecuted a case at Tywyn magistrates' court on 4 August 1899. This time, Richard Rowlands, a quarryman of Ratgoed, admitted obstructing the guard,

David Fred Price, in the execution of his duty and assaulting him, and expressed regret. Dix said that he did not want to be hard on the defendant but wished to stop the practice of obstructing the company's employees; the details of the obstruction were not described in the *Cambrian News* report. Rowlands was fined 1s on each charge, and costs, a total of £1 7s 6d. Dix's appearances saved the company the cost of appointing a solicitor.

A case heard at Machynlleth on 27 September 1899 was probably similar. John Benbow, a blacksmith living in Esgairgeiliog, was charged with having ridden in a carriage in contravention of the regulations and assaulting David Thomas, the Machynlleth station master. Benbow insisted on attempting to travel on the platform between the compartments of the 7.20pm departure when the seats there were already occupied and refused to take a seat in a compartment. He was removed to a compartment but got up as soon as the train started. The train was stopped and when Thomas approached him he struck him in the face. The train was delayed twenty minutes before he was removed. In the witness box, Benbow said that others travelled on the platform, he had a ticket and should be allowed the same privilege. He had had some drink and was afraid of being sick if he went inside, adding that he was an Englishman and 'they had got it in for him'. He was fined 5s for the assault and 1s for the contravention, plus costs, total £1 3s. Told he would remain in custody until the fines were paid, he managed to raise the money, presumably from friends in the public gallery, for one of the fines, and was told to pay the remainder later that day. 'This [the] defendant, who was by this time thoroughly frightened, promised to do.'

In August 1899, Dolgelley Rural District Council had served notice on the railway to abate a nuisance caused by its manure heap, calculated to weigh about fifty tons, affecting the stream in Corris. Dix replied that he was not surprised at the smell arising from the river, but it was not caused by drainage from the stable but from 'filth continually thrown into the stream and from privies directly emptying into [it]'. There were no sewers in the village. The council resolved to take proceedings unless steps were taken to remedy the complaint within seven days. At Tywyn magistrates' court on 1 December, Dix said that the manure had not been removed because he had no place to remove it to but gave an undertaking to remove it once a fortnight.

No doubt all this legal activity, as well as the normal day-to-day minutiae involved in running a small railway, had contributed to the need for an advertisement placed in the *Montgomery County Times* on 15 April 1899 and repeated the following week: 'Clerk wanted, with knowledge of railway accounts and shorthand preferred.' Applicants had to supply three testimonials in support. No details of any appointment have survived but it seems unlikely that anyone with knowledge of railway accounting and shorthand would have been looking for work in rural Montgomeryshire.

Socially, Dix hosted a public dinner at the Braich Goch Inn on 29 September for employees as a reward for the contribution towards making 1899 a record year for the railway, at the invitation of the board of directors, the *Montgomery County Times* reported, although none of them attended. Another account suggests that the dinner was an annual event, but no other reports have been found.

In a speech, the vicar, R.J. Edwards, recalled the days of horse haulage: 'In those days, it seemed almost like a hideous dream, people were cooped up in something worse than a horse box. A hole, which let in the rain and gave no light, served as a window and the passengers were so cramped in this pretence for a carriage which creaked and groaned and wriggled about that when they arrived at their destination they scarcely knew whether they were in or out of it. The permanent way, too, was in a fearful condition, the rails were simply old tram rails, many of them projected several

inches above the others, and twisted about in such a variety of ways that, as a rule, the carriages ran off the line three times before reaching Machynlleth (laughter). On other occasions when many slate trucks were attached to the train the passengers often assisted the poor horses up the incline (renewed laughter). That was the state of things about 20 years ago.'

Responding with a wide-ranging speech, Dix commented on the Cambrian services at Machynlleth, noting that passengers taking the 11.15am departure from Aberystwyth did not reach the town until 2.30pm, over three hours to travel twenty-six miles.

On 7 October 1899, Dix was partially successful with a new appeal to the rating assessment committee. The railway had been revalued three years before but the basis was wrong, he claimed. The committee upheld the valuation but agreed to a reduction on the railway between Aberllefenni and Alltgoed, 'over which there is not much traffic.'

High spirited employees ensured that guard Evan Griffiths's wedding to Mary Lewis was remembered on 11 October 1899. A train passing the bride's home 'just as the wedding party arrived' set off detonators, while the 12.45 departure left with continuous whistling to start the happy couple on their way to their London honeymoon.

In close communities, like those of Corris and Machynlleth, recruitment ought not to have been a problem but the *Montgomery County Times*, 30 December 1899, carried an advertisement seeking a porter and an engine cleaner: 'must be strong and sober men. Apply saying age and wages required.' The advertisement was repeated on 20 January 1900. On 14 July a porter and horse drivers were required.

Changing social mores were reflected by a correspondent to the *Montgomery County Times* on 21 April 1900, published in full: 'Taking advantage of the cheap tickets to Corris on Easter Monday, I was glad to find the little Corris Railway again the pioneer in progress, once more showing that they study the comfort and convenience of their passengers. This time it is the smokers who will all be delighted to know that the "smoking" compartments are now labelled for their sole use and benefit. All smokers when travelling by rail know that it is the usual custom for ladies and children in arms to select a smoking compartment to travel in to the disgust and exclusion of lovers of the weed. Those ladies who do so on the Corris line, do so at their grave peril, as the smokers' privileged compartment is labelled in bold letters, "Men only. Smoking."'

Over one hundred years later it would be expected that a correspondent wishing to make a similar point would take a completely opposite view.

Two cases of refusing to show tickets when requested had different outcomes when heard sequentially at Tywyn magistrates' court on 4 May 1900. John Williams, a quarryman, had refused because he had had to stand from Machynlleth to Esgairgeiliog; he said the company had broken its contract to provide him with a seat. The magistrates decided that a technical offence had been committed but dismissed the case. Robert Edwards, another quarryman, had refused to surrender his ticket until the train stopped, when he did so. His solicitor asked for the case to be dismissed but although the magistrates found that a technical offence had been committed here too, they fined him 6d plus 9s costs. Unless the reporting was defective, did the magistrates not realise that their decision-making was inconsistent?

Evan Thomas and Thomas Vaughan, otherwise Jones, were sentenced to three years at Bradwell reformatory school, Sandbach, Cheshire, when they admitted stealing 2s 3d in copper from Machynlleth station on 14 May 1900. Thomas said that Vaughan had persuaded him to break the window and Vaughan blamed Thomas. Both had convictions for felony.

Unable to reach a settlement with W.H. Long MP over the land at Pont Ifans, despite agreeing to a draft conveyance as recently as May 1900, the case returned to court, this time in the Queen's Bench Division of the High Court on 4 August, a Saturday. Long's demands had been so exorbitant, it had been impossible for the railway to accept them, its barrister said. One of the judges said that the land partially occupied by part of the cottage was of no use to anyone and the best thing for Long to do would be to grant a 999-year lease for 2s 6d a year to acknowledge his ownership. After some discussion, he suggested that the company should pay £25 plus costs for the freehold. The absence of further references to the dispute suggests that a resolution was found.

Notwithstanding Dix's efforts on behalf of the company, in the twentieth century the directors seemed to cool towards him. It had been his practice to take leave at the end of April each year. In 1901 however, he was told that this was not convenient, but, 'later on the managing director would send one of his assistants to Corris to take charge during the manager's absence.' Despite increased responsibilities, after George Owen, the engineer, had died in 1901 he had taken on the obligation of signing the engineer's reports, despite his lack of qualifications for doing so, and had signed as locomotive superintendent since at least 1885, probably doing so since his appointment, again despite a lack of qualification, his request for an increase in salary in August 1902 was refused. In March 1902 he had been ill, his condition considered serious, and requiring an operation in April, reported the *Cambrian News*.

On the board, Samuel White was elected a director on 26 March 1902, resigning as secretary. William George Verdon Smith, secretary of the London United Tramways, George White's nephew, replaced him.

Dix and the railway came under criticism from Corris residents and the local authorities throughout 1902. They wanted a train to connect with the Cambrian's 7.50am departure from Machynlleth, otherwise it was not possible to get from Corris to Tywyn for the magistrates' court before midday. Replying to a letter from the Tywyn magistrates, he said that it was not practical to run an earlier train, and suggested they should induce the Cambrian to change its timetable.

There were also complaints about the fares, about the level crossing in Corris, which could be closed for up to fifteen minutes when the quarrymen were trying to get home for their dinner, and the lack of separate carriages for quarrymen. A public meeting held in the village on 18 August agreed to get up a petition. On 26 November, the directors resolved to ask Dix for his opinion before replying. He had already told the council that he would take action to minimise inconvenience at the crossing.

In January 1903 the *Cambrian News* reported that a 'most unsatisfactory' answer to the petition had been received. However, on 10 February the directors considered it again, resolving that the fares could not be altered and that, 'inasmuch as the winter service of trains was now in operation, the grounds of complaint as to the time of running the morning train were removed.' No more was said.

Dix was not the only employee who contributed to the community. On 18 December 1902, driver William Roberts was presented with a clock to mark his recent marriage to Annie Evans and in recognition of his services as organist at Capel Salem.

Abercwmeiddau quarry took a unilateral decision to withhold some of the money it owed the company towards the end of 1903, claiming that the charges were excessive. The quarry was told that the rates were defined by Parliament and, 'that unless they adopt a more reasonable attitude, prepayment of any freight for conveyance must be insisted upon.' No more was said about this either.

In December 1903, Dix told the directors of a large rock fall at Braich Goch, warning that slate volumes would be reduced as a result. A year later, White reported that he had been communicating with Dix about decreased traffic receipts and that Dix, 'had promised to use his utmost efforts to try to substantially reduce the decrease before the end of the year.' Revenue for the year, at £4,000, was only £381 less than in 1902, while expenditure was reduced by £409. A 6% dividend was declared.

The employees had paid tribute to Dix's twenty-five years with the railway on 19 December 1903. In a ceremony in the waiting room at Corris he was presented with an illuminated address. The directors were probably unaware of the landmark achieved by one of their employees. Dix and his wife celebrated their silver wedding with a party at the village school attended by some eighty persons.

Two of the directors received titles during this period. George White became a baronet, adopting the designation 'White of Cotham House', in Bristol, in the birthday honours list announced on 24 June 1904; Robinson received a knighthood a year later.

Dix clearly had no problem with his leave application in 1905, for on 2 May he, his wife and a friend, sailed from Liverpool to New York on Cunard's RMS *Caronia*, arriving back at Liverpool on the White Star line's RMS *Cedric* on 27 May.

A sudden death brought criticism to the railway after Anne Mary Playfer, a 60-year-old woman holidaying in Aberystwyth, died in the Cambrian's Machynlleth waiting room on 11 July 1905. Ascending the steps from the Corris station after a visit to Talyllyn, she had complained of feeling unwell and died a few minutes later. At the inquest the next day, a doctor attributed her death to heart failure, suggesting that she had exerted herself and ruptured an artery.

The *Cambrian News* report attracted a letter, saying that it was as well the railway was only seven miles long, otherwise there would be more deaths. Entering one of the 'miniature tramcars with glass all round' felt like entering an oven, with foul air, excessive heat and enough noise to shatter the nerves of the strongest, and the beautiful scenery could not be seen or enjoyed from the train. A better way to visit Talyllyn would be to spend a few hours enjoying Machynlleth and then to take a coach, enjoying a, 'beautiful drive that cannot be surpassed by anything in the Lake District.' Hotel keepers should be encouraged to run charabancs, the writer concluded.

Ten years after the railway had been held accountable for the death of a horse because of its poorly maintained fences, it was in court again. Despite months of prevarication by Dix, Mary Owen of the Braich Goch Inn won her claim for £3 for two sheep killed by a train when it came to Dolgellau county court on 11 December 1905. The sheep had met their maker on 1 April. In court there was some debate about whether they had breached a railway fence or had first escaped onto the road before finding their way onto the railway. The judge found that the evidence that the railway fences were defective, denied by Dix and a ganger, was substantiated by the postman. Asked for leave to appeal, the judge replied that it would be much cheaper to repair the fences.

Evan Griffiths, the guard whose marriage was celebrated in 1899, found himself before Tywyn magistrates' court charged with the theft of an 11lb lump of coal, value at 2d, on 6 April 1906. The offence had occurred at Aberllefenni. Griffiths, who had fathered three children, admitted the offence, saying that he had no explanation for it. His solicitor, who provided his services without charge, asked for the case to be dealt with under the First Offenders' Act, as Griffiths had an excellent character. The case was dismissed on payment of 5s damages and 14s costs. Surely anyone whose life would be improved by a 2d lump of coal would struggle to deal with a 19s penalty?

Another employee, Howell Davies, a station master who lived at Fridd Gate, appeared before the Tywyn magistrates on 7 September 1906, to face a charge of having in his possession a spear for catching or killing salmon. Caught by gamekeepers at Pantperthog, Davies offered them money. He had been warned about poaching before. His solicitor successfully argued that a spearhead, which Davies had surrendered, could not

be called a spear without a handle. The offer of bribes appears to have been overlooked and he was fined 13s including costs.

Youthful pranks and petty vandalism brought eight youths before Machynlleth magistrates in January 1907, charged with a breach of railway bylaws. A porter asked them to leave when he found them at the station on 2 December, a Sunday, when there were no trains, but one of them became aggressive and another used 'filthy language'. Dix said that he did not wish to 'press the case unduly' but had to make a gesture; there was often damage found on Mondays, with wagons moved and points tampered with. The charges were dismissed and the lads severely reprimanded by one of the magistrates, who extracted a promise that they would not misbehave again. They had gone to the station after attending Sunday school. (At the same court, incidentally, six youths were fined 1s each for throwing snowballs in the street.)

It is a rare year that the Dyfi does not flood at Machynlleth, blocking the roads to Aberdyfi and Corris at least once. Since 1859 many of the newspaper reports said whether the railway was also blocked, or remained passable. After the river flooded four times in two months in 1906 pressure on the authorities to take action was given prominence by a letter from the vicar of Corris, R.J. Edwards, published in the *Cambrian News* on 23 March. Describing the inconvenience, he described the poor state of the footpath between the town and the river, saying also that the former Corris Railway arch under the Cambrian line was 'unspeakably filthy … a *latrina*'.

A month later he was supported by Edward Griffiths, who called for the road to be raised, saying that the railway's booking office had also often been subject to flooding and that in response the railway's formation had recently been widened and raised. The councils should follow the railway's example, he concluded. Not mentioned elsewhere, the work on the formation was probably carried out by the

THE DOVEY IN FLOOD

A typical Dyfi flood scene, viewed from the cliff top above the Cambrian Railways station. The Corris Railway's route has been highlighted, the line ending at the point where the railway crosses the river.

railway's own labour. Although the road was eventually raised, the problem was not eliminated, and it is only as this book was being written, more than 100 years later, that plans were made for a new bridge and modified road layout to address it. Where it survives, the railway embankment is up to 16 feet wide and 20 inches high, constructed of slate waste with edge-set slate edging and slate coping, a technique that would protect it from the regular floods.

The railway's own bridge was replaced for the second time during 1906. Dix had first been given approval to repair it in November 1902, but either any work done was of a limited nature or nothing was done, for in October 1905 Robinson, 'reported the necessity for re-constructing the bridge over the river Dovey.' Dix sought tenders for the construction of three coffer dams via an advertisement in the *Cambrian News* on 23 March 1906 and they, and those for the materials, were considered on 16 May. Contracts were awarded to Dorman, Long & Company Limited for the steelwork, £412, and John Chidlaw Roberts, timber merchant, for the piers, £465.

In October, Robinson forecast that the bridge would be completed in two to three weeks. Ironically some timber was washed away from the site during a flood early in November, but on 29 November the *Aberystwyth Observer* reported its completion, attributing its design to the versatile Dix. 'It is,' said the paper, 'an ornate and substantial structure of decidedly neat design ... a steel girder bridge of four spans of about 50ft each, resting on dressed stone piers, with concrete foundations, and capped with Yorkshire stone. The stones for building the piers were from the Aberllefenni quarries.'

Occasionally railway customers would request a reduction in their rates. Ratgoed's request in October 1906 had been refused but Aberllefenni coal merchant William Hughes's application for a reduction dealt with on 17 December 1906 brought about Dix's dismissal, for Hughes claimed that he was being overcharged because the manager was also trading in coal. Asked to explain himself, Dix admitted to being a shareholder in the Corris Coal Company,

The third Dyfi bridge, seen from the south bank. (John Scott Morgan collection)

The 'new' bridge, in situ long enough for plants to become established on the right-hand pier, with a double-headed train posed for the benefit of the photographer; it carries no passengers. The leading loco has lost its displacement lubricator.

Seen from the downstream side, a short train crosses the 'new' bridge in 1926. The clerestory roof of the middle carriage was appreciated by passengers for its increased headroom and improved ventilation. (J. Valentine)

the extent of his participation not being recorded.

Having obtained further information from Dix in January, on 28 May 1907 the directors resolved to dismiss him, paying him £50 in lieu of three months' salary.

John James O'Sullivan was appointed to replace him, with a salary of £250. Born in Crosshaven, County Cork, in 1849, O'Sullivan was well qualified for the position, having just retired on pension from the Cork, Blackrock & Passage Railway, where he had been its accountant for several years before being appointed general manager in 1885. It is quite likely that he and Robinson were already acquainted as the latter had been manager of Cork Tramways from 1873-5.

Always named as J.J. O'Sullivan in notices and the press, he moved with his wife and two of his four daughters to Aberystwyth. Not speaking Welsh, he could not engage with the community as Dix had done, but he did become active with the Cambrian Resorts Association to encourage tourism.

The delay between the issue with Dix being raised and the dismissal/appointment may be accounted for by

the need to find a replacement. Hughes's request for a reduction in rates appears to have been overlooked.

O'Sullivan's first moves were to advertise the railway, 'miniature gauge, bijou saloon carriages', in the *Aberystwyth Observer* and to start discussions with Cambrian Railways on the issue of combined tickets from Cardigan Bay resorts on Sundays, the latter attracting the wrath of local clergy when word got out. A meeting held to protest at Machynlleth town hall on 11 July 1907, *Aberystwyth Observer*, 18 July, was attended by an audience that included six clergymen. What grated about the prospect of Sunday excursions was they would be run, 'not because there was any necessity or as an act of mercy, but merely in order to cater for pleasure-seekers and pleasure-loving people, and anybody who might go to the neighbourhood.'

One speaker said that he had been brought up in a puritanical household which had been very gloomy on Sundays but he, and his audience, had outgrown some ideas about Sundays. They all agreed though that Sunday should be a day of rest, especially for those engaged in manual labour. He cited a speech made by the

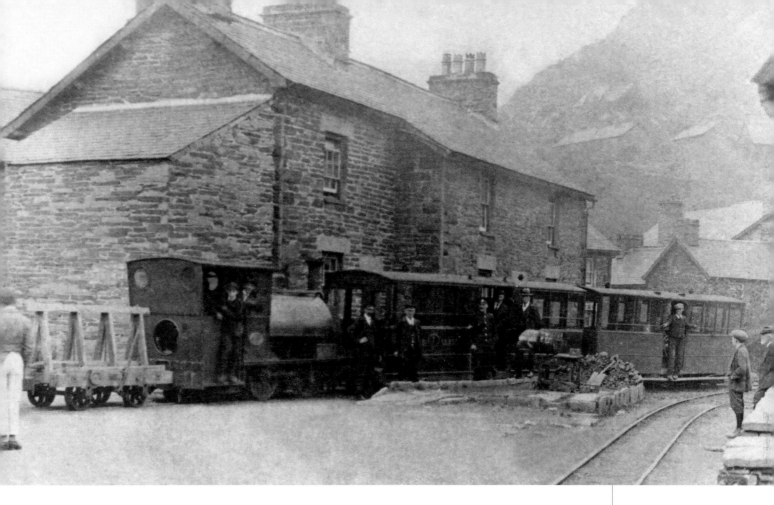

A train from Aberllefenni passes the Corris 'coal yard'. The bearded man leaning on the wall on the right could well be Dix, the railway's energetic manager from 1879 until 1907.

historian Thomas Babington Macaulay when a Factory Act had been in Parliament, who said that the nation was richer because Sunday labour had been abandoned, man laboured on Monday better equipped intellectually, full of corporeal vigour as well as cheerfulness.

Two speakers had experienced Sundays in Germany and France, they said; after early morning service, religion was flung to the winds and people abandoned themselves to all sorts of labours and pleasures. In contrast London on a Sunday was calm and peaceful. Another had experienced Sunday excursions in South Wales; their object seemed to be to defeat the Sunday Closing Act. Allowing Sunday trains in Machynlleth would be the thin end of the wedge to the introduction of 'continental Sundays' in Wales. No mention was made of the Cambrian's ordinary Sunday service, presumably because it did not cater for pleasure-seekers and pleasure-loving people. A 'comprehensive resolution', carried unanimously and sent to the directors of the railway companies concerned, seems to have deferred the evil day for the time being.

When the royal commission into the workings of the Sunday Closing Act 1881 had met at Welshpool in September 1889, incidentally, the commissioners had been told that only 19 of 400 quarrymen consulted at Corris had favoured the Act's repeal and that the village's tradesmen were 'practically unanimous' in their support of it.

Joseph Richards Dix, from a newspaper photograph taken not long before his dismissal.

A short train in front of the 'new' station, although signs of wear on the roof suggest that it was not that new when the photograph was taken. The glazed light above the open door is lettered for the station master's use. Manager J.J. O'Sullivan established his office in this building, commuting from his home in Aberystwyth. (Kingsway Series)

No 1 with two carriages at Machynlleth on 29 June 1909. Notice the differing detail to the underframes and glazing of the carriages. (H.L. Hopwood)

In December 1907, the *Welsh Gazette* said it thought the church leaders had been hypocritical on the subject when it noticed workmen installing Machynlleth's new sewage system working on Sundays without any objection being raised. The Free Church Council seems to have given up on its 1903 objection to the Vale of Rheidol Railway running Sunday trains, but was still protesting about the Corris Railway's Sunday operation, and the Cambrian Railways' sale of cheap Sunday excursion tickets, in 1909.

O'Sullivan also oversaw completion of the replacement station building at Machynlleth, which had taken several years to bring to fruition. In March 1903 the town council's sanitary inspector had complained about its insanitary state and poor condition, the council and Talyllyn parish council both passing resolutions about it. The *Cambrian News*, 8 May 1903, editorialised, 'What is the use of telling the company that their neglect is under the consideration of the council? The company should do what is necessary without force, but if force is necessary, force should be applied forthwith. The public are about sick of the Corris Railway Company.'

Dix had responded to the council's threat to take action about the privies in June 1903 by closing them, but the directors did sanction the building's replacement at the same time. A year later, the Cambrian Railways dealt with a letter from him, which set the scene: 'Our station at Machynlleth, owing to a variety of causes, has been allowed to become very dilapidated. It was originally very badly built without any pretence as to design or elegance and quite in the wrong position. There is no space for proper platform accommodation, and sidings are very cramped and inconvenient. My directors have given me permission to erect new station buildings, but to carry out this properly and to remodel our platform and sidings it is desirable that we should have another portion of your field adjoining … We have some land …

which originally formed part of our line to Derwenlas and which was abandoned on the opening of the Cambrian line. This latter piece of land is of no use to us, but as it adjoins your property my directors have agreed to my offering you this strip in exchange for the portion of the field now required, … I may say that the land is not fenced off, but if you agree to the proposed exchange we will put up a suitable fence or remove the present fence to the new boundary …'

The Cambrian accepted the proposal, as well it might; the land it received covered 1,360 square yards, while that given up amounted to 782 square yards.

Expenditure on the new bridge and the station was not recorded against the railway's capital account, the last expenditure under this heading being recorded in 1901, as shown in the table.

Capital Expenditure 1885-1901

1885		Cr	Dr
	Increase in value of horses		£4 5s
1886	Waggonette		£20
	Depreciation in horses	£10	
1887	Waggonette		£18
	Depreciation in horses	£9 10s	
	Horse sold	£20	
1888	Horse sold	£16	
	Depreciation in horses	£4	
1889	Dog cart and harness		£31 17s 6d
	Two horses		£48
	Depreciation in horses	£18	
1891	Waggonette		£6
1892	Two horses		£50
1894	Expenditure on horses		£57 12s
1896	Lines open to traffic, new stables, buildings, etc		£333 9s 8d
	Horses		£9
1897	Lines open to traffic, buildings, etc		£63 3s 2d
	Horses		£47
1898	Lines open to traffic, buildings, etc		£45 6s 6d
1899	Working stock		£6 3s 6d
1901	Lines open to traffic, buildings, etc, working stock		£90

On 19 September 1907 the *Aberystwyth Observer* noted that the station was approaching completion, saying, 'The new structure is admirably situated and will contain several rooms for the use of the public.' Since O'Sullivan had taken charge of the railway, it said, 'several improvements are to be noted as less time is lost at the stations en route.' The identities of the station's architect and builder are unknown but with those of the Festiniog, Lynton & Barnstaple and the Isle of Man Railways it is ranked amongst the most attractive of the buildings on British narrow-gauge railways. O'Sullivan established his office in it; Dix had worked from home.

A fare increase for children attending Machynlleth county school, from 1s per week to 2s 6d, was another of O'Sullivan's initiatives. In response to objections, his offer of charging £1 per quarter was accepted on 27 December 1907, although the headmaster remarked that *pro rata* it was higher than the Cambrian Railways' charge.

Legally, 1908 was a busy year for the company, with three claims resulting in writs being served on it. The first claim, considered in February, was made by Williams, Jones & Company of Corris for the non-payment of invoices rendered for the supply of coal in April and June 1907, total £38 13s 1d. Having discovered that Dix was a partner in the company, the directors were reluctant to pay. Counsel's opinion advised that it was liable but could claim for the profit made because of Dix's involvement. The Corris Coal Company appears to have been a trading name for Williams, Jones. The claim, with a counter claim by the company against Dix, was heard by the official referee in London on 22 February 1909.

Dix gave evidence that the company had not been disadvantaged by his participation in the coal supply and had approved it by letter in 1880. Judgment, with costs, was given against the company but deferred pending an appeal. It was probably abandoned.

The second claim was Dix's own, considered on 27 April 1908. He wanted £25 for furniture that he said he owned and £7 10s for rent to the end of 1907. The company believed that it owned the furniture and asked for proof to the contrary and responded to Dix's claim for six months' notice to terminate the office tenancy by saying that it had been terminated by his dismissal. It agreed, however, that rent had been paid up until June and the office had been used until October, offering to settle for £5. Dix replied, via his solicitor, that he could substantiate both claims and would settle for £32 10s.

The third claim, discussed on 28 July, was from Roberts, the Dyfi bridge reconstruction contractor, who sought £126 2s 1d for building coffer dams to protect the new piers during construction. The company argued that they had not been necessary and had been made without authority. The case had started in the High Court and had been sent for arbitration. Heard by Basil Mott on 9 July, Roberts was awarded £83 18s plus costs. 'It was believed that there are good grounds for an appeal but in view of the comparatively small amount at stake it was not considered worth the company's while to incur the expenses of further litigation.'

Dix appeared to have had little rapport with the directors under White's leadership. Even before that, most contact was by letter but there was a directorial visit to Corris most years and he did occasionally attend board meetings. Despite telling him off occasionally, the pre-White directors would also acknowledge when they thought that he had performed well. He must have worked hard at running the railway, for he had no clerical support. His account books and records had been subjected to unannounced auditors' inspections in 1898 and 1906, when everything had been found in order, so financial impropriety was not an issue.

Under White's chairmanship, he was refused leave and a pay rise. Robinson probably never visited Corris, although Dix did sign an illuminated address presented to him on the occasion of his [Robinson's] silver wedding anniversary in 1899. From a twenty-first century perspective it would seem that he had a claim for wrongful dismissal. The *Cambrian News*, 7 June 1907, recorded his departure as a 'great surprise'.

Dix had served the company for twenty-eight years. He left Corris, the contents of his house, *Bryn Awel*, were advertised for sale in *Y Negesydd* on 23 April 1908, and underwent theology training at Bangor before taking a church appointment at Rhosneigr, Anglesey, where he stayed until May 1915.

Dix's community status had resulted in a portrait, complete with photograph and a verse about the railway, one of a series on Welsh notables, being published in *Papur Pawb* (*Everyone's Paper*) on 2 June 1900. Despite being born in Somerset, he had, it said, many Welsh characteristics, was compassionate, contributed to eisteddfodau, organised events, encouraged temperance, preached, lectured, and served as a parish guardian, a National School guardian and on diocesan committees.

In Corris, he seems to have been regarded as an unelected civic leader. One of his events, held in the school on 10 November 1888, had been a concert for the benefit of the village poor, raising over £20. The room was 'crammed to excess' and he had performed a 'humorous comic song' and a ballad himself. On one occasion he executed a will and on another he acted as a substitute 'father of the bride' at a wedding.

A member of the Bangor Diocesan School Association's governing body from 1900, he gave his occupation as 'lay reader, Church of England' in the 1911 census. Still supporting his wife and two daughters, he lived at Gwynant, a substantial eight-roomed semi-detached house with views of the sea, a very different environment from Corris. Dying in Lymm, Cheshire, on 20 October 1927, his estate valued at £2,192 4s 3d, he was buried with his wife at St Llonio's, Llandinam, Montgomeryshire.

Joseph Richards Dix, the Corris Railway's energetic manager for so many years, was buried in Llandinam, close to David Davies, the railway builder and colliery owner, and other members of his wife's family. The inscription for Dix himself is partially obscured by the turf.

The company's only legal expenditure in several years was £50 in 1909, which could be the costs element of Roberts's claim, if the award was allocated to maintenance. The company lost all the claims brought against it in 1908.

Dix's dismissal coincided with a change in the railway's fortunes. From 1893 until 1903 dividends had been 5% or higher. In 1904 4% was paid, followed by 1% in 1905. Profits insufficient to pay a dividend were made in 1906-8 and in 1909 a loss was made for the first time. Thereafter minimal profits were made on only three occasions during the remainder of the company's existence. Given the railway's debt being carried by Imperial Tramways, £4,756 in 1909 rising to £18,216 in 1930, the payment of dividends appears to have been a pointless exercise. It might have been a sop to Imperial shareholders which was no longer required under the White regime. With a degree of unwarranted optimism, Imperial always showed the railway's debt as an asset.

Sir James Clifton Robinson, managing director of the Corris Railway Company from 1892 until his death in New York in 1910, was buried in the Kensal Green Roman Catholic Cemetery in north-west London, where this fine memorial was erected. A newspaper account of his funeral reported that his hearse was followed by thirty carriages and that by the time the last of these had arrived at the cemetery the graveside obsequies had been completed.

The lack of directorial activity from 1909 may be related to Robinson's retirement in February 1910. With an extraordinary career in tramways, including building the Highgate Hill cable tramway, the first in London worked by mechanical power, and the electrification of London United Tramways' system, another London first, his Corris role was a mere footnote. He died on a tram in New York on 6 November 1910, aged 62, his death the subject of numerous reports and obituaries. Returned to England on the White Star liner *Majestic*, his body was conveyed from Plymouth to London in a carriage attached to the GWR's Ocean Express. With O'Sullivan among the mourners, a requiem mass at the Church of the Immaculate Conception, Mayfair, was followed by burial in St Mary's Roman Catholic cemetery at Kensal Green. His estate was valued at £13,641 6s 9d; he had previously made provision for his widow and son; the White brothers were his executors.

Robinson was replaced as a director by solicitor Hugh Greenfield Doggett, a Bristol solicitor, but the managing director role was not continued. Apart from complying with their statutory obligations the directors seem to have given up on the railway.

In the absence of board minutes, O'Sullivan's letter book covering the period from 1908 until 1915, which survives at the National Archives, gives an understanding of the railway from its manager's perspective. In 1908 he had been keen to negotiate through rates to main line railway destinations. The quarries had been pushing him for reductions but any concession that he made would be insignificant without a contribution from the larger companies. He wrote to the LNWR and the GWR saying that the Cambrian had told him that it could do nothing without their agreement. As an example, he thought the rate from Machynlleth to Birmingham, 8s 9d per ton for 108 miles, was biased against his customers when compared with the rates from Porthmadog, 9s 7d/155 miles, or Blaenau Ffestiniog, 8s 9d/119 miles. If the rate was calculated proportionately, then from Machynlleth it would be 7s 11d based on the Porthmadog rate or 6s 8d based on Blaenau Ffestiniog.

He had been told that Ratgoed and Cymerau would be developed if the rates were better and the new owners of Braich Goch, which was closed, wanted better terms. Persisting, in September he sent the Cambrian a petition from the quarry owners, saying that if the Machynlleth rate was improved he was prepared to recommend a single rate, including transhipping at Machynlleth, for all the Corris area quarries, except Llwyngwern, to his directors. Llwyngwern, being closer to Machynlleth, would not stand being charged a general rate that was appropriate for Corris and Aberllefenni. He proposed that the main line companies tried a 10% rebate for 12 months to encourage the business. It is unlikely that the GWR and the LNWR would want to disturb the status quo and equally likely that the Cambrian would be aware of this and its response to O'Sullivan was to fob him off.

Despite its recent reconstruction, the Dyfi bridge still required close observation. Low water in August 1908 revealed that the stone protecting the northern side of the bridge piers was not performing as required, so O'Sullivan had railway personnel reinforce it with rough concrete. In December scouring around the western sides of the piers occurred after flooding; on this occasion O'Sullivan had stone available for reinforcing as soon as the water level fell although he thought that more concrete would be required.

Rhiw'r Gwreiddyn was a small slate quarry half a mile south of Esgairgeiliog. Despite that proximity, it was never rail connected, its output being taken to Machynlleth by road. In 1908 O'Sullivan informed Robinson that he had managed to get the traffic by carting the output to Esgairgeiliog, a measure that required double handling. To avoid this he had asked Kerr, Stuart, better known as locomotive builders, about supplying a 'road waggon' capable of carrying a rail wagon between the quarry and the railway. Such a wagon would also be useful at Machynlleth and Corris, he said.

Getting a price of £12, he ordered one, only to be told that the price was £32. Obtaining quotes for similar vehicles from Stagg & Botson, T.C. Aveling and Buck & Hickman ranging from £28 to £35 3s 8d he cancelled the order, telling Robinson that as the prices were so similar it was obvious that a mistake had been made and there was no point in trying to enforce the contract. He then obtained a road trolley that could be carried on the wagon from the disused Hendre Ddu quarry for £4 10s. He was building a wagon to carry the trolley, he said, and anticipated completing the project for about £12 in total.

Lineside timber at two locations was dealt with in December 1908. Sixty-nine larch trees growing at the foot of an embankment were bought for £14 10s to be used as telegraph poles and sleepers. Many of the line's telegraph poles, noted O'Sullivan, were in poor condition. He had also noticed that the site bought by the railway from Long at Pont Ifans in 1900/1 had been included in a plot offered for sale for timber. He had got the auctioneer to withdraw it, requiring Robinson to produce the deeds to support his contention that it was railway land.

The transfer of £1,976 to the capital account under the heading of 'lines open for traffic, buildings, etc' in 1908 was no doubt a retrospective allocation in respect of the Dyfi bridge reconstruction and the Machynlleth station building which were not otherwise accounted for.

Some of the railway's money was kept in a bank account in O'Sullivan's name. Writing to Robinson about the accounts in January 1909 he explained, 'The balance shown on this account is in reality the property of the Corris Company though lodged in the bank in my name, and I propose leaving a signed cheque in my safe so that the account can be transferred at any time without troubling my executors, should I unpreparedly and unfortunately be compelled to take a longer journey than I ever did during my railway career without a return pass.' His precautions were for nought, because in the event of his demise and the bank being aware of it the cheque should have been refused.

The directors obviously thought it was a suspect arrangement, for on 2 April O'Sullivan informed Robinson that the account had been closed and a new one opened in the name of the Corris Railway No 2 account.

It was the practice of railway companies to exchange free travel passes for use by senior officers and directors. In February 1909 O'Sullivan informed Robinson that he had received passes from these companies: Cambrian, Brecon & Merthyr, Cheshire Lines Committee, Rhymney, North Wales Narrow Gauge, Bishop's Castle, Vale of Rheidol, Lancashire & Yorkshire, Talyllyn, Festiniog, Cork, Bandon & South Coast, Cork, Blackrock & Passage, Tralee & Dingle and Great Western. His use of the last was restricted to the route between Aberystwyth and Carmarthen. Courtesy of the Cambrian, CLC and the LYR, he could reach the English east coast but not London. To use his Irish passes the Cambrian and GWR would have got him to Carmarthen from where he would have had to make his way to the Cork ferry at his own expense. Similarly, he would have had to pay for the journey across Ireland to reach the Tralee & Dingle Railway.

A fire occurred at Maespoeth shed on 8 May 1909. The carpenter arrived there at 7am and found one of the rafters on fire. He managed to extinguish it before help arrived from Corris. It was believed that sparks from the loco that left the shed at 6.10am were responsible. O'Sullivan thought the damage would cost £5 to repair and solicited £2 compensation to replace the carpenter's damaged clothes.

The opportunity of acquiring some little-used rail, the same section as that used on the tramways, was taken by O'Sullivan in August 1909. The source was Cambergi quarry, near Aberllefenni, then closed. The railway had no stock and it was available for £2 10s per ton, 'practically old iron price.' The quarry had had a tramway about 4-500 yards long, a short section on the flat and a long incline.

O'Sullivan put some effort in to marketing the railway's scenic attractions and commissioned a poster printed in two colours. The issue for summer 1909, dated June, was illustrated by three engravings based on photographs and a map that highlighted the railway and the Talyllyn coach routes. The timetable showed connections from locations as far away as London, both Euston and Paddington.

Despite the poster stating boldly 'no Sunday trains', a Sunday service was started in August 1909, two years after the idea was first mooted. O'Sullivan had persuaded the Cambrian to offer through tickets to Talyllyn, telling Robinson that, 'I have succeeded in getting in the thin end of the wedge with regards to Sunday passenger working.' Once again, the Free Church Council objected, appealing for those responsible, 'to reconsider the matter … to refrain from proceeding with a movement which

is so utterly at variance with the long-established custom of the neighbourhood, and opposed to the highest interests and truest welfare of its people.'

It is unlikely that the council would have expected O'Sullivan's reply: '… at present I cannot see my way to comply, but if your council can succeed in getting the other companies to discontinue the running of Sunday trains and cheap excursion tickets to other places than Talyllyn lake, the owners of motor omnibuses and horse vehicles, etc trading in competition with this company to abandon their services, assist the local quarry owners to increase their output and reopen the quarries now closed, I would be prepared to place the resolution before our managing director (Sir Clifton Robinson) for his favourable consideration. I may add that your aid in this direction would be appreciated, and would prevent the possibility of the line being closed for passenger traffic and only worked for mineral purposes, as the present revenue is only slightly in excess of the working expenses.'

In his covering letter to Robinson, whose name and rank he would regularly drop into his correspondence with others, O'Sullivan referred to the possibility of withdrawing the passenger service. It was a contingency that he hoped was remote but which he would consider if motor bus competition became more severe. He would have to see what savings would be made and if profits could be made on the mineral service at the current levels of income. He had made the comment, he explained, because he was aware that the community had become alert to the inconvenience caused by the closure of the nearby Mawddwy Railway to passengers in 1901 and for all traffic in 1908; it was soon to be reopened.

He concluded saying, 'I also had in view our proposed extension to Talyllyn Lake and Abergynolwyn to join with the Talyllyn line to Towyn.' O'Sullivan had promoted the idea of an electric railway linking the neighbouring lines to Robinson in July 1907 but there is no evidence that it was taken seriously; there was certainly no application for powers. The Cambrian declined to offer through tickets for Sunday services in subsequent years.

Producing the draft accounts for 1909 in January 1910, and seeing a loss of £210, led O'Sullivan to submit a detailed report to Robinson. Passenger traffic was affected by the weather and 'road motor coach' competition from Barmouth and Aberystwyth to the extent, he estimated, of £100. The local population was declining, leaving many empty properties and affecting local traffic. This also affected goods and parcels receipts as did competition from road carriers.

The slate trade was poor. Braich Goch was still closed, Rhiw'r Gwreiddyn and Era were working in a small way; they could sell all their slate but lack of capital hampered development. Aberllefenni and Ratgoed showed slight increases. Output from Abercorris and Llwyngwern was down, in the latter case due to the bridge that connected the quarry to the railway collapsing. Although total tonnage was reduced by 177 tons, revenue was increased by £15 5s 3d because of the better rates obtained from Rhiw'r Gwreiddyn and Era; their slate travelled a shorter distance.

Part of the Upper Corris branch was re-sleepered, the first time in twenty-five years that any work had been carried out on it. The Ratgoed Tramway had needed repairs and the main line had required 380 sleepers and fastenings. To economise on traffic expenses, he had reduced staffing levels, decreasing wages by £192. On paper but not in fact, the loss was the railway's first.

The locomotives had been allowed to become run down. It had been difficult to keep them going in 1907/8, and although more expenditure had been required it should not be needed again for some time 'if the engines are properly looked after'. Wagons had also required expenditure. Work was done on all three loco boilers by Brush, apparently at Loughborough. Repairs on No 1 included a copper patch under the firehole door; they all needed copper stays and brass tubes replacing

and new steel plate in their coal bunkers. The boilers of Nos 2 and 3 were lifted out of their frames and a quantity of bolts replaced.

At Maespoeth extensive repairs were carried out on No 3, including repairing its pony truck, remetalling axle boxes and replacing piston rings and rods, valve spindles and quadrant blocks. Less extensive work was carried out on Nos 1 and 2. £507 4s 4d had been spent on loco running expenses during the year, compared with £414 7s 5d in 1908. On the capital account £99 had been allocated to 'working stock', some of which would have been for upgrading a 3rd class compartment to 1st class and building a 'small iron wagon'.

O'Sullivan dealt with a letter from Dix on 2 February 1910, the latter having learned that retired railway officers qualified for privilege (quarter) fare tickets and requested ticket orders for himself and his wife to travel from his new home at Rhosneigr to Afon Wen and Porthmadog on 8 February. O'Sullivan refused the request, telling Robinson: 'I enclose application received from Dix … If he was a retired officer in the ordinary way he would be entitled … I do not consider that he is entitled to any personal favours either from myself or the company.' A similar request a year later was also refused, prompting Dix to request an explanation; there is no record of any response.

The idea that Dix thought he should be treated as a retired officer raises questions about the way his dismissal was carried out. Robinson had been 'requested to formally dismiss Mr Dix' but on 1 July 1907 reported that he had sent his representative, accompanied by O'Sullivan, to take charge of Dix's records. In 1907 Dix was 58 years old; was he led to think that he had been compulsorily retired rather than dismissed? If Cozens's account (see bibliography) was dependent on folk memory, as seems likely, then there was no recollection around Corris of Dix being dismissed when he was researching in the 1940s.

To deal with road competition for passengers O'Sullivan decided to run an

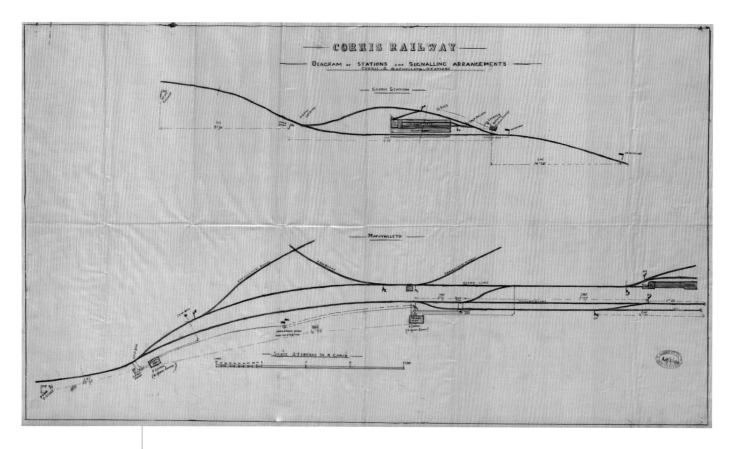

O'Sullivan's plan submitted to the Board of Trade in 1910, showing the track layouts and signalling arrangements at Machynlleth and Corris. (National Archives)

extra train in connection with an extra on the Cambrian, writing to the Board of Trade on 21 February 1910 that he wished to divide the line into two sections, splitting it at Corris. He would then work the Machynlleth-Corris section with the staff and telephone. Deputed to deal with the request, Colonel Edward Druitt minuted that he could not understand it, whether O'Sullivan wanted to run one train after another combining staff and ticket working with absolute block and using the telephone instead of the block telegraph, or merely wanted to cross trains at Corris. It would be best if O'Sullivan met him with plans of the signalling arrangements or else Druitt would 'go over the line with him'.

The meeting took place in London on 2 April (Saturday!) and Druitt agreed to O'Sullivan's proposal. The line was already worked in two sections, Machynlleth-Corris and Corris-Aberllefenni. The first had a red staff with Annett keys for Llwyngwern and Esgairgeiliog sidings and the key for the Maespoeth cabin, which was kept locked and the signals not used.

The second had a blue staff with Annett keys for Fronwen and Mathews Mill sidings and the loop at Aberllefenni.

With Druitt's approval, the railway's operating rules were amended, dividing the line into three sections: Machynlleth-Maespoeth Junction; Maespoeth Junction-Corris and Corris-Aberllefenni. The signals at Maespoeth and the Maespoeth Junction-Corris staff were not to be used and the key for the cabin was attached to the Machynlleth-Maespoeth Junction staff. Rules dealing with the train staff and signalling by telephone were added.

Maximum loadings were now defined: for a single locomotive, four carriages and a van; two engines coupled together, eight carriages and a van. The rule about train working, 'The number of coaches to be decreased as the traffic gets light daily, and when possible one coach only to be worked without the van', was maintained.

The working timetables for 1909/10 show the locomotive leaving Maespoeth at 5.20am and the departure of the first train from Corris to Machynlleth at 5.35am.

Trains were shown as 'mixed', 'pass' and 'G&P', the last without explanation, possibly passenger trains carrying merchandise. In 1910 the 9.05am and the 2.15pm from Machynlleth to Aberllefenni and the 8.00pm from Aberllefenni to Corris were indicated thus. Only the 5.35am and its return from Machynlleth to Aberllefenni were timetabled to run mixed. The service was arranged so that it could be worked by a single locomotive.

O'Sullivan told Robinson that the new arrangement meant that he could run more trains, or specials, when required. In addition to the extra train being run on the Cambrian, a motor tour to Dolgelley was to be operated that the GWR was expected to promote in Bala, Corwen and Llangollen.

It was clearly time to modernise the Talyllyn coach service with modern motor coaches. He told the Cambrian's agent that the distance from Corris to Dolgelley was twelve miles: 'I think with a good coach we could do it in an hour.'

He was right to be cautious about the motor vehicles. Bristol could not supply him. A London company had its vehicles on hire to the War Office and could not make one available until 17 August 1910. A Sheffield company refused to make an agreement because it thought it would not be paid if the weather was poor and the service unprofitable. For this year O'Sullivan had to continue using horses.

In June 1910 he had sold a mare for £4 10s; she was 5 years old when purchased in 1892. He did not propose to buy any more horses if he could get charabancs. A horse called Captain was to be sold for £9 in January 1911; he had a cataract in one eye and O'Sullivan thought that he would sell the horse before his other eye was similarly afflicted.

At 31 December 1910 the railway owned the following road vehicles: 2 charabancs; 4 wagonettes; 1 dog cart; 2 brakes; 1 landau; 1 cart and 1 road trolley. It also owned eleven horses. In addition to the rolling stock that featured in the statutory returns, the railway owned three platelayers' trolleys. How the charabancs

listed here, in O'Sullivan's annual return, fitted in with those he was trying to hire earlier in the year is not understood.

The slate traffic showed no improvement. Braich Goch was still not at work and in July 1910 the lessee at Llwyngwern went bankrupt, owing £5 1s 9d for one month's traffic. O'Sullivan told Robinson that he held five wagons and a slab truck as security, they were in fair condition and worth considerably more than the debt.

On 31 March 1911 O'Sullivan thought that he would try his luck with securing a royal visit to the railway with a letter to Lord Herbert Vane-Tempest. Following the forthcoming investiture of the Prince of Wales at Carnarvon on 13 July the King and Queen were to be his lordship's weekend guests at Plas Machynlleth. Offering to lay on a special train, O'Sullivan wrote, 'I am building a nice new carriage, and would push on its completion, so as to have it ready … I could take them up to Corris or Aberllefenni and back in about an hour and a half, and would not object to doing it after church on Sunday if you thought well of it.' He also offered the use of two new motor charabancs if required. Lord Herbert obviously did not 'think well of it' although the royal party did partake of a motor drive to Corris and Talyllyn, returning via Towyn and Aberdyfi.

The rolling stock return contained in the annual report to shareholders reveals that during 1911 the number of composite 1st/3rd class carriages was increased by one, to four, while the stock of 3rd class carriages was reduced by one, to two. Expenditure on 'repairs to rolling stock' of £142 10s 10d, compared with £60 the year before, indicates that the 'new' vehicle was converted from an existing one.

The new charabancs were those to be hired from, and newly built by, the Bristol Tramways & Carriage Company for the summer season. O'Sullivan's user-requirement was quite demanding: seating capacity 20 minimum, speed 19mph, capable of climbing gradients of 1 in 7 to 1 in 14 and with sufficient brake power to park on those gradients.

In the years until the outbreak of the war, O'Sullivan put a lot of effort into promoting the road services and the company reaped some rewards from them. 'So far, the motor coaches are a complete success,' he informed White on 13 September 1911. In addition to the Talyllyn service, circular tours were run in conjunction with the Cambrian and the GWR, with the charabancs making the link between Corris and Dolgelley, and excursions were run from Aberystwyth.

The vehicles used were usually new 22-seat charabancs that travelled to Wales by rail. To get an operating licence from Aberystwyth Corporation he had to resort to subterfuge because the council would not give him a licence as the manager of the Corris Railway. He therefore applied in his own name as a resident of that town. Garages were rented in Dolgelley from 1912 and in Aberystwyth from 1913.

In 1913 two charabancs were driven to Wales for use on the Corris/Dolgelley services. To the £52 18s 11d profit they made O'Sullivan added £58 railway revenue. Aberystwyth services made a profit of £236 17s 3d. O'Sullivan's table contains more information for 1913.

Vehicle	Route	Miles	Receipts	Passengers	Receipts per passenger	Receipts per mile
AE 2767	Aberystwyth, several routes	6,024	£622 5s 7d	7,515	19.8	24.7
AE 2553	Corris, Dolgellau	1,767				
AE 3180	Talyllyn, Abergynolwyn	2,154	£430 13s 5d	4,596	22.5	19.3
AE 3184	Talyllyn, Abergynolwyn	1,363				
AE 3184	Aberystwyth	289	£289 8s	271	21.9	20.5

YN LAKE AND PASS, CORRIS RAILWAY MOTOR COACH 801

One of the motor charabancs arrives at Talyllyn. (Donald George)

With two exceptions, all of O'Sullivan's correspondence with Bristol from 1911-5 dealt with the guide book or the road services. The exceptions were an attempt to persuade White to join a consortium investing in the quarries on 10 August 1912 and a brief note on 11 January 1913 commenting on the reopening of Abercwmeiddau and reviewing the state of the quarries. The last letter, dated 15 September 1915, dealt with the termination of arrangements for renting a garage at the Waterloo Hydro Hotel in Aberystwyth because the vehicles had been commandeered for the war effort.

O'Sullivan's attempts to expand the railway's tourist market in December 1911 had brought him up against inter-railway politics. He had visited Charles L. Conacher, the Cambrian's traffic manager, with a view to securing that company's participation in a tourist brochure. Conacher made clear his opinion that the Cambrian already produced an adequate supply of such literature and that O'Sullivan's efforts were resented. As the Cambrian also objected to the railway issuing tourist tickets to Corris from other parts of the country O'Sullivan realised that the other companies would not support the idea either. The railway had been publishing guidebooks since the mid-1890s and was to publish another in 1912.

Reviewing the period from Dix's dismissal in 1907, it appears that O'Sullivan could have done more to reduce costs, at least by reducing train mileage. Although the number of passengers carried fell by 4,000 in 1907, passenger train mileage increased by nearly 10,000 miles. In 1898, the railway's best year, 14,300 miles were run to carry 83,044 passengers. In contrast in 1908, O'Sullivan's best year, 25,718 miles were operated to carry 60,164 passengers. Goods train mileage, on the other hand, did reflect the traffic more accurately. When mineral traffic fell to a third of what it had

A passenger train viewed from over the fence near Llwyngwern in the 1920s.

been in 1905/6 the mileage was halved and remained at that level.

During the war, the railway saw little change. Unlike the main line companies it was not taken over by the government, and the requisitioning of motor vehicles forced those who wanted to travel to use the trains. In 1915 38,229 passengers were carried, just over 10,000 fewer than in 1913. 4,668 tons of slate carried represented a reduction of 2,312 tons compared with 1913. By 1920 losses had risen to £4,208.

Fatalities were avoided when the locomotive hauling the 11.30am train from Machynlleth derailed near Abergarfan, between Fridd Gate and Llwyngwern, and turned on its side. The *Cambrian News*, 11 February 1916, which did not give the date, said the carriages, fuller than usual because some passengers were going to a funeral, remained upright and there were no injuries. The loco crew also escaped injury, jumping off in time. Some passengers continued their journey on by motor vehicles, others on foot. Traffic was dislocated for the rest of the day and O'Sullivan did what he could to minimise the inconvenience. He should have reported the accident to the Board of Trade too.

Cozens (see bibliography) gives the date of the incident as 9 February and says that there were two carriages carrying about twenty passengers, in which case it was about half full. He added that the permanent way foreman thought that a heavy snowstorm half an hour before the accident might have played a part in it. Whatever the cause, it did nothing to ease the railway's locomotive availability position. It had been 16-21 years since any of them had received works attention and they were becoming run down.

Concerned about the amount of effort required to deal with the Board of Trade's returns for no apparent purpose, on 22 June 1917 Frederick Harrison Withers, company secretary, sought permission to cut out some of the statistical minutiae from the annual reports, citing the need to save labour and paper. 'The cost of issuing such elaborate accounts is out of all proportion in the case of a railway with a total revenue of less than £2,000 for the year.' And for a company with only one shareholder, he might have added. He got the approval he needed after a civil servant had recommended, 'This unimportant, uncontrolled, narrow gauge railway may probably be allowed …'

Two deaths in 1916/7 brought more changes to the railway's management and direction. Firstly, Sir George White died on 22 November 1916 and was replaced by his son, Sir George Stanley White, the second baronet, as a director and by Samuel White as chairman. As a mark of mourning, the Bristol office used letterheads printed with black borders.

O'Sullivan died on 21 April 1917, aged 68, following several months of declining health and a bronchitis attack. His obituary, *Cambrian News*, 27 April, said that he was well liked and had a genial character. Despite his age he had been one of the first to enrol with the Aberystwyth Volunteer Corps. After a service in the catholic church, he was buried in Aberystwyth cemetery, Corris Railway employees acting as pallbearers. His effects were valued at £822 5s. Withers took on his responsibilities as manager and with the Cambrian Resorts Association.

The records are incomplete for these years; the most likely sequence of events was that H.C. Godfray resigned earlier in 1917, leading to Verdon Smith's election to the board and Withers' appointment as secretary. Godfray had probably resigned because of ill health; he died after an operation on 21 May 1918. Previously, H.G. Doggett had died on 11 April 1915 and been replaced by James Henry Howell, a Bristol businessman. One of his executors was Sir George White.

In Corris, Withers's agent was David Thomas, Machynlleth station master, appointed principal clerk. This arrangement lasted until March 1921 when Daniel James McCourt, an Irishman previously employed by the Middlesbrough Tramways Company, was appointed manager.

Judging by newspaper reports, or the lack of them, the railway had not been much affected by the war. There were no reports of employees being called up or volunteering to fight, although Richard Emlyn Richards was granted an exemption

By the time of his death on 21 April 1917, J.J. O'Sullivan had decided that as he had enjoyed his time living in Aberystwyth he would be buried there, rather than in Ireland, his birthplace. His grave is in the town's Plas Crug cemetery.

on personal grounds and because of his employment by the railway in 1916. When he was called again in 1918, Withers told the Machynlleth Rural Tribunal that the company was applying for another railway protection certificate and his case was adjourned. The outcome is not known, nor is the position that Richards held on the railway.

In November 1917, *Y Llan* had reported that the railway was very generous to convalescing troops from the Voluntary Aid Detachment hospital at Machynlleth, providing free travel to a social function at Corris and a special train to take them back.

Although the railway was still nominally the owner of three locomotives, they had become run-down and it had been a long time since it had been able to put all three, or even two, into service. Indeed, on 5 September 1919 the *Llangollen Advertiser* reported that, 'Train service on the Corris Railway was suspended for some days last week "owing to the breakdown of the engine!"'

'Stand over there and I'll take a picture of you with the train,' some time during the summer of 1922, the 'Tattoo' 0-4-2ST about a year old. The user specification given to Kerr, Stuart & Co overlooked the railway's unusual, for narrow gauge railways, use of rolling stock with side buffers, and the maker's standard design for buffer beams was insufficiently deep. Ever resourceful, the railway resolved the issue by fixing heavy timber planks to the beams. This photograph disproves the claim that the locomotive's chimney was broken by striking a bridge when it entered service.

In contrast to the experiences of other railways, post-war passenger traffic came back to its 1910 levels, around 50,000 passengers. There was more variation in goods traffic but it was 1927 before it fell below 6,000 tons, the level of 1912. Fare increases imposed on railways in 1917 were responsible for fare revenues increasing by around £400 annually but, of course, inflation had increased costs. Mileage, though, started off at 15,150, 5,000 less than in 1913, but steadily rose, with only two exceptions, to 22,457 by 1929.

The fall in slate traffic, 1,000 tons less in 1926 than in 1925 and then another 1,000 tons less in 1927, apparently followed an attempt to raise the rates. Braich Goch responded by buying a steam lorry to transport its output to Machynlleth. The Upper Corris branch consequently fell out of use in July 1927.

The railway's loss carried forward into 1922 had increased by £1,703, mostly a consequence of the purchase of a new locomotive, a Kerr, Stuart 'Tattoo' 0-4-2ST, delivered in June. The losses, subsidised by Imperial Tramways, had reached £6,830. There was also an overdraft, £536 in 1922. Imperial showed the debt at £12,773.

Made slightly smaller than the standard 'Tattoo' design because of the railway's restricted loading gauge, the new locomotive had been ordered in November 1920. Delivered painted in War Office grey livery and equipped with vacuum brakes, it immediately became the mainstay of the railway's operations, its arrival making possible a remarkable feat of engineering with limited resources.

From 1918 to 1929 the railway employed Albert Edward Hulme as engineer at Maespoeth. There he dismantled Nos 1 and 3 and reused the best components to erect a new locomotive. The work took several years, the combined loco known as No 3 as it had that loco's cab, with number plate attached, although it probably contained more of No 1. The extent of the work went unnoticed until the Talyllyn Railway dismantled it in 1986 and found that it had frameplates from two locomotives. Leaving the railway at around the time the GWR took over, Hulme returned to his mother's house in Manchester, an arrangement that cost him his marriage, as his wife and his mother did not get on.

The Tattoo about to leave Aberllefenni for Corris, c1924. (John Scott Morgan collection)

Quite early in its career, the Tattoo cracked its chimney, most likely by running into a fallen branch, and a clamp was attached to keep the loco in service. This view, taken at Machynlleth, shows the clamp and damage done to the smokebox by the loco being overworked. It also shows the deflectors fitted to the saddletank to keep water out of the motion.

Seen at Machynlleth in August 1928, the Tattoo's chimney has been replaced while its smokebox has been subject to extensive repairs; it was replaced with the boiler in 1929.

The Tattoo after its 1929 boiler had been installed. Electric train lighting had been installed, the connector for bunker-first running being located on the far side of the buffer beam.

Since 1921 the railway had been the only 'tramway' under Imperial's control, the company functioning as an investment vehicle with a large holding in the Bristol Tramways & Carriage Company and some other investments under its control. The railway was therefore surplus to requirements. In January 1924 Verdon Smith, acting for Imperial, approached the GWR and offered to sell it for £10,000. In return, he offered, Imperial would undertake not to run road services in Wales.

Inspecting the line, GWR officers said that they found it, permanent way and rolling stock, in good order. Observing that the railway had powers to run road services, they noted that it owned two 32-seat charabancs and a 6-seat motor wagonette, eight horse-drawn vehicles, two horse-drawn goods vehicles and five horses. More information about the company's financial position was required to establish the value of an offer. This point was repeated at the end of the year but nothing came of the proposal.

In July 1928, the railway and GWR entered into a non-compete agreement, whereby the times of the railway's omnibus service between Aberystwyth and Machynlleth would not conflict with those of the GWR and both companies agreed not to undercut each other's fares.

The relationship became much closer after the GWR was approached by the accountant Sir William McLintock Bt with a proposal that it acquire the late Sir George White's controlling interest in the Bristol Tramways & Carriage Company, and the railway, early in 1929. In addition to owning the Bristol tramways the Bristol company also operated an extensive bus network in competition with the GWR and the London, Midland & Scottish Railway. On offer was 53% of the voting capital, 72% of the issued capital, now held by White's trustees. An intriguing aside revealed that while the company had been paying 7% dividend for several years it also had considerable undeclared profits, which affected its valuation. McLintock's successors are part of the KPMG financial services group.

A portrait of the Tattoo at Machynlleth. The train lighting cable connecting loco and carriage can be seen behind the vacuum brake pipe.

Albert Edward Hulme, the Maespoeth-based engineer from 1918 until 1929, at Aberllefenni with the Tattoo in 1925. No doubt he was responsible for the deflectors and the chimney clamp as well as the work he did to combine two of the Hughes locos into one.

Hughes No 3 as it was returned to service by A.E. Hulme, at Machynlleth in 1928. (E.A. Gurney-Smith)

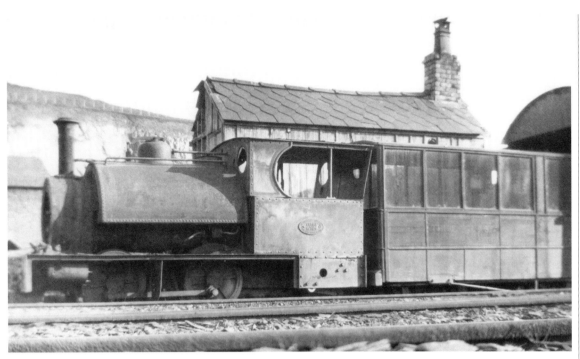

Hughes No 2 at Machynlleth on 16 April 1927. Some parts, including the smokebox door and some of the motion, had probably been removed for reuse on No 3. It is quite likely that the loco had been pulled out for the photographer's benefit. (I. Higgon)

No 3 in action near Llwyngwern soon after it had re-entered service in 1928. The train formation includes the clerestory-roofed carriage. (B.B. Edmonds)

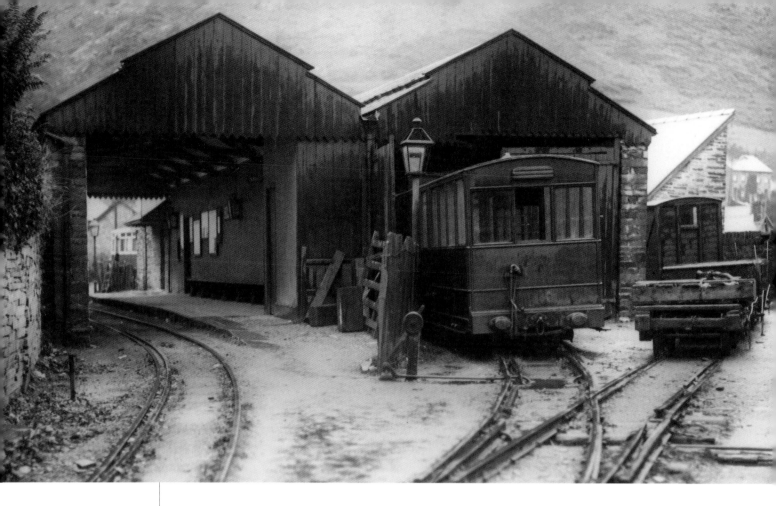

Corris station as the GWR representatives would have seen it in 1924. The railway did well to get a station with running line, platform, two carriage shed roads, a bypass road, and, later, a stable block and coach store, into such a restricted site. Of course, it did not have to make provision for the ubiquitous use of the motor car, but a motor bus can be seen beyond the platform.

At a meeting with McLintock on 4 February 1929, the GWR's assistant general manager John Milne made it quite clear that his company was not interested in the railway 'at any price'. By the end of the meeting, however, he had agreed to recommend the purchase of the railway for £1,000 in conjunction with the purchase of the Bristol shares.

Meeting on 6 February, Sir Felix Pole, the GWR's general manager, and McLintock agreed that the GWR would take over the railway from 1 March 1929 and that Imperial would discharge its liabilities when the purchase was completed.

Meeting for the first time since 1909, on 27 February 1929 the directors transferred Imperial's £15,000 ordinary Corris Railway stock from nominees to the company itself. An unexplained transfer of debentures made on the same occasion probably had the same outcome. Verdon Smith chaired the meeting and his co-directors were Sir George Stanley White and Sydney E. Smith. Samuel White had died on 29 November 1928 at the age of 67. The fourth director

listed in the 1928 annual report was Sidney E. Baker, a solicitor.

Although no money had changed hands and much needed to be done to put the takeover into effect, McLintock was anxious to complete the transaction, saying that the GWR had been effectively in control of the railway and responsible for its expenses since 1 March. The GWR, of course, could not take over a railway without the approval of Parliament but it could make an investment so on 18 July 1929 it agreed that the purchase money would buy the shares and the debentures rather than the railway. The records do not reveal the circumstances of Imperial agreeing to advance £600 to the railway to keep it going on 5 April, the money to be refunded by the GWR.

The takeover strategy was in place by 17 September 1929. With the four Imperial directors remaining in office for the time being, retaining their qualifying shareholdings, £13,000 ordinary stock would be transferred to the GWR on payment of £808 6s 5d. The transaction was itemised thus:

£15,000 ordinary stock	£7 6s 5d
£5,000 debenture stock	£200 0s 0d
Repayment of advance made by Imperial to the Corris Railway on 5 April 1929	£600 0s 0d
Remainder of debt due to Imperial by Corris Railway	£1 0s 0d
Total	£808 6s 5d

To reach this valuation McLintock had worked backwards, starting by taking the value of stocks and stores, £1,100 15s 6d, adding the amounts due to the railway, £576 12s 2d, to the agreed purchase price of £1,000 and subtracting the current liabilities, £2,369 1s 3d, giving £208 6s 5d. He then suggested how it should be allocated. With the nominal payment of £1 to Imperial, the railway's accumulated losses of £15,844 7s 4d would be written off.

The stocks were transferred to Sir S. Ernest Palmer, a GWR director, and F.R.E. Davis, the GWR's company secretary, jointly as GWR nominees. The GWR's cheques were posted to McLintock on 19 November 1929 and Imperial's receipt for the reimbursement of the advance and its statement assigning the debt were issued the next day. The transfers of £13,000 ordinary stock and £5,000 debentures to the GWR were registered on 26 November 1929.

The Tattoo running round a train that includes the clerestory-roofed carriage, Machynlleth 1925. (John Scott Morgan collection)

CHAPTER 3

RAILWAY COMPANY OWNERSHIP

The first recorded GWR involvement with Corris Railway operational matters occurred on 19 December 1929 when the GWR's locomotive committee agreed to the reconditioning of No 3, 'the cost of the work to be borne by the Corris Railway Company.' This arrangement was not mentioned in the correspondence dealing with the sale. No 3's loco history sheet shows that it had been at Swindon since 28 November; it was returned to work on 22 April 1930, the overhaul being costed at £512. The loco's boiler history shows that since 1926 it had used a boiler built for No 1 in 1914; the GWR put it back to work with second-hand tubes. It was not given any of those features traditionally associated with the GWR, brass number plates or copper safety valve bonnet, for example, either then or later, and in that way the Corris fleet, such

A nice portrait of No 3 at Machynlleth a few months after it had returned from Swindon in 1930. The sloping cab backsheet appears to have offended the aesthetic sensibilities of the GWR engineers who dealt with the loco, for they replaced it with one that required a little more metal. Because the work was nominally carried out for the Corris Railway Company, the front lamp bracket was moved from the buffer beam to the top of the smokebox but not replaced with a GWR standard fitting. The guard is uncoupling the loco from its train. Although there is little to show it, this is a rare image of a Corris Railway passenger train operated under GWR auspices. (R.G. Jarvis)

A few years later, the fireman's side of No 3 on view as the loco prepares to leave Machynlleth with a short goods train. The vacuum brake pipe has been removed.

On shed at Maespoeth after the GWR takeover, the Tattoo now equipped with GWR standard lamp brackets. (John Scott Morgan collection)

Perhaps concerned that the quarries might misappropriate them, the GWR appeared to be more enthusiastic to claim ownership of the Corris wagons than it did the locomotives. Here, both wagons are loaded with coal, although the timber-bodied vehicle, on the left, was nominally for general traffic.

as it was, was treated differently from the remainder of the GWR empire.

The Great Western Railway Act of 1930 received the royal assent on 4 June that year. In addition to authorising the transfer and vesting of the railway in the GWR it also ruled that Corris Railway officers would not become officers of the GWR and that the Corris Railway Company would discharge any obligations due to them.

John Milne, by then the GWR's general manager, wrote to his heads of departments on 11 July 1930, instructing them to 'take the necessary steps to bring this undertaking within the organisation …' and informing them that it had been agreed that the services of D.J. McCourt, the railway's manager, 'should be dispensed with' and that ganger Thomas Griffiths and porter J. Jones would be retired before the GWR took over.

The last recorded business of the railway's directors had taken place on 13 March, when the last general meeting had been held, the only one recorded in the minute book. At the end of June, a GWR official collected the company's deeds from Bristol. The company's seal is

displayed with those of other amalgamated companies at Swindon's Steam museum of the Great Western Railway.

McCourt had lived in Machynlleth while running the railway. Although his dismissal on the GWR takeover may appear rough, he became deputy permanent way engineer of Bristol Tramways during 1930 and was promoted to be permanent way engineer in 1933. He died after a short illness on 31 January 1939, aged 45. The list of insurances in force when the GWR took over, incidentally, included one for a motor car that he had used.

In the short term, the GWR made a loss on the Bristol purchase. Not wishing to own more than 50% of the company, it sold the surplus shares over three months from April 1930 at prices several shillings less than the £1 10s it had paid. At the end of the year though, it received a 10% dividend on its holding.

On reflection, Imperial had been good to the Corris Railway, a benevolent owner. Given the same results, the railway could not have maintained its losses had it been dependent on the goodwill of ordinary shareholders.

A line of 1-ton capacity wagons at Machynlleth in March 1946. The three on the right have wooden bodies.
(J.I.C. Boyd)

An iron wagon with end doors at Corris. There were two of these 1½ ton-capacity wagons, nominally used to
carry locomotive coal to Maespoeth. Both are still extant.

The goods brake van with a 1-ton wagon at Machynlleth. The van and the wagon chassis are preserved on the Talyllyn Railway. Withdrawn with the carriages in 1930, the passenger brake van was slightly larger. (John Scott Morgan Collection)

Twice a year, Imperial shareholders were told that the railway had earned enough to pay a dividend while overlooking the renewals and other expenses paid for by the parent. It was sufficiently well equipped for the services it offered and the paucity of tales about derailments or breakdowns, despite the ongoing battle to replace sleepers, suggest that maintenance was more than adequate. Indeed, the railway's tramway origins had bequeathed its locomotives with treads half-an-inch narrower than the norm, making track precision essential, as the Talyllyn Railway found out in the 1950s, when it had to store No 3 for twelve months until its track was fit for it to run on without derailing.

There was one constancy through the Imperial years that dated to the railway's

earliest days – the auditor's report on the company's final accounts was signed, just as all those preceding it, by J. Fraser, the practice started by James Fraser, the only individual to be involved with the original Corris, Machynlleth & River Dovey Tramway and the Imperial era. With the sale of its largest assets, Imperial had no function so on 12 May 1930 Sir William McLintock was appointed to liquidate it.

The railway was deemed to be included in the GWR from 4 August 1930, the date its account with the National Provincial Bank at Machynlleth was closed and the balance paid to the GWR's account with Lloyds Bank at Oswestry. For administrative purposes it was placed within the GWR's central Wales division, which also had responsibility for the

Vale of Rheidol Light Railway and the Welshpool & Llanfair Light Railway.

Notwithstanding the earlier expenditure on No 3, 4 August 1930 was also the date that it and the Kerr, Stuart were taken into GWR stock as Nos 3 and 4. The latter had been unnumbered previously; its works plate was altered to include the number. A local scrap dealer had disposed of Nos 1 and 2 at Maespoeth in 1930.

In the meantime, on 24 July 1930 the GWR's engineers' department had recommend £2,000 be spent on general repairs, the work carried out not being recorded. Later, on 27 November 1930, the traffic committee resolved that the railway's passenger service should be withdrawn from 1 January 1931. There was no explanation for this decision but the massive fall in passenger numbers and revenue in 1930 (19,502/£390) compared with 1929 (52,455/£1,080) following the introduction of a competing

service, by the GWR, must have been relevant. The possibility of the 1930 figures being for a part year cannot be ruled out either. The carriages built by Metropolitan in 1898, Nos 7 and 8, were sold into non-railway use at Gobowen and the remainder were condemned at Swindon on 22 December 1930.

Corris Railway carriages absorbed into GWR stock

Corris No	GWR No	Type
1	6215	Composite
2	4993	3rd
4	6216	Composite
5	4991	3rd
7	6217	Composite
8	4992	3rd

At a meeting of the law, parliamentary and estate committee held on 12 February 1931 it was agreed to buy the freeholds of two

A gap in the GWR numbering scheme permitted No 3 to retain its old number. The previously unnumbered Tattoo became No 4. Rather than supplying standard GWR-style brass number plates, the locomotive's works plates were altered to show the number.

Before the decision was taken to withdraw the passenger service in 1930, two of the carriages were taken to Swindon and one of them stripped down. (John Scott Morgan collection)

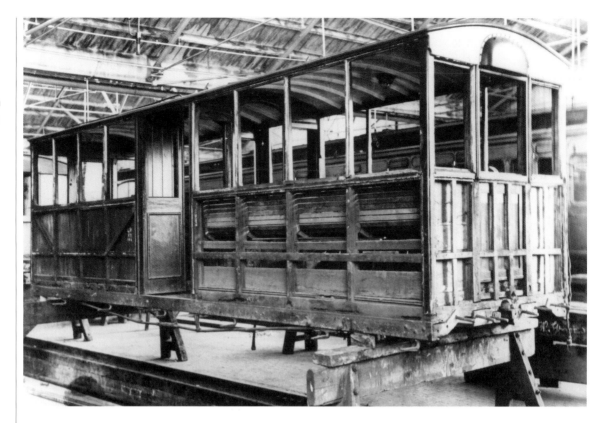

Corris Railway wagons in the throes of dismantling at Swindon in November 1930. The cost of getting them there must have been greater than the value of any material recovered for reuse. (Museum and Galleries of Wales)

plots at Corris previously leased from the Marquis of Londonderry. The purchase, for £420, included the right to take water which had previously cost £1 annually.

Under the new regime, the GWR's station master at Machynlleth oversaw the railway day-to-day operation. Although the traffic and revenue data was no longer required to be separately accounted for and published, the Corris Railway Society was, with support from Welshpool & Llanfair Light Railway Preservation Society members, able to obtain records from the Cambrian's Oswestry headquarters before it was closed.

There were only three quarries using the railway, Aberllefenni, Ratgoed and Cymerau, the first supplying most of the traffic, 2,219 out of 2,442 tons in 1934. It was owned by A. Hamilton Pryce, whose father had objected to the carriage of passengers in 1879. The GWR reduced the rate from 5s 5d per ton to 3s 9d and then to 3s 3d, initially linked to an obligation to ship a minimum of thirty-six tons per week that was not maintained. There was still a small amount of coal and merchandise traffic to be had but the greatest issue was road transport.

One of the things that the GWR did with its £2,000 allocation was to replace the McKenzie & Holland signal arm with one of its standard pattern. Seen in 1939, the abandoned route of the Upper Corris Tramway has been lost in the boscage.

Four bogie carriages at Machynlleth. From the left they are No 6, No 8, No 5 and No 7. The latter is 3rd/1st, the others all 3rd. No 6 was built by Falcon in 1888, the others by the Metropolitan Railway Carriage & Wagon Company. The bars along the windows enabled the guard to pass along the train checking or selling tickets while it was in motion. (John Scott Morgan Collection)

A pleasant scene of No 4 captured during a break in shunting on a summer's day at Machynlleth. (Martin Fuller collection)

No 4 shunting goods stock at Machynlleth in July 1933. (J.E. Simpson)

No 3 at Machynlleth in 1930, after the GWR had equipped the locomotive with a bracket capable of taking side-mounted lamps, and before it had finished branding the wagons. (S.W. Baker)

An uncommon view of a Corris loco running light engine. No 3 passing Llwyngwern, 1930s.

Looking very smart, No 4 stands at Machynlleth with a short goods train in April 1936. The bicycle in one of the wagons was probably not revenue earning traffic. (Martin Fuller collection)

A Caernarvon-based wholesaler who took twenty tons per week from Aberllefenni got a same-day service when he sent a lorry from Machynlleth to collect and deliver it. The best the railways could do, in a coordinated attempt to get his traffic in 1936, was three days. Thanks to the intransigence of the quarry employees who undertook the transhipment at Machynlleth, some 36 hours of the journey was spent within 10 miles of the quarry.

In 1935 Pryce had sold a seven-year lease on Aberllefenni to Henry Haydn Jones, the local MP and owner of the Bryn Eglwys quarries and the Talyllyn Railway. Edward Thomas, Jones's manager, told the GWR that the Corris rate should be minimal or even eliminated if it meant that the traffic was secured for rail throughout, but to no avail. Nevertheless, the railway remained in business and even increased its traffic in 1940 and 1941, carrying slate to repair bomb-damaged properties. Then the government decided that repairs should be deferred until the war ended and that was the beginning

of the end for the railway. Until then the only noticeable way that it had been affected by the war had been in 1942 when the Upper Corris branch had been lifted for scrap.

With 1,000 tons lost in 1942 and again in 1943, when it just scraped over 2,000 tons, operations were reduced to three days a week in October 1943. A strike in 1947 brought about the loss of the Aberllefenni traffic, the GWR being deterred from closure by the Machynlleth station master assuring Paddington that prospects would be good when the quarry reopened.

It was perhaps fortunate that the locomotives were not too taxed by the work expected of them and they rarely troubled their owners for if there had been a catastrophic failure the railway's future would have been at risk. It was 25 June 1940 before No 4 required sufficient attention to warrant a visit to Swindon, where an intermediate overhaul took 71 days. Earlier, light repairs had been carried out on it over a 45-day period from 19 August 1930.

No 3 heads through Aberllefenni loop with a train comprised mainly of slab wagons in 1939. (A.E. Rimmer)

No 4 approaches Aberllefenni on 20 March 1939. (H.B. Tours)

No 4 shunting wagons across the station entrance in Corris on 20 March 1939. (H.B. Tours)

No 3 starts away from the level crossing at Pont Ifans in 1939. (A.E. Rimmer/ John Scott Morgan collection)

No 3 was returned to Swindon for an intermediate repair taking 49 days on 17 September 1942, the last time that any Corris loco made the journey to Wiltshire. Subsequently, work was carried out at Machynlleth, on No 4 from 4 December 1944, 93 days, No 3 from 3 July 1945, 22 days, and No 4 again from 9 December 1947, 43 days. After less than four months back in traffic it was taken out of service on 6 May 1948.

Whether the work carried out at Machynlleth was undertaken on Corris metals or whether the locos were put on a wagon and taken over to the standard gauge shed is not known. Taking the number of days out of traffic in the GWR era, No 3 (216 days against No 4's 252 days) seems to have benefitted from its initial trip to Swindon, but it might not have been used as much as No 4. The mileage recorded for No 3, 64,341 miles,

is unlikely to be that worked since 1878. Since 1930 it represents just 3,500 miles annually. The 198,566 miles recorded for No 4, on the other hand, could easily be its mileage since new, 7,354 annually, twice as much as No 3. If No 4's recorded mileage was accrued only since 1930, then it averaged 11,031 miles annually, three times that of No 3. Either way, it is no wonder that it required more time out of traffic and failed to see the end of the Corris service.

In the end though, it was the weather that did for the Corris Railway. Heavy rain during August 1948 aggravated the scour near the Dyfi bridge, leading to a decision to stable the loco, only No 3 was working, at Machynlleth in case the bridge was damaged. The out-of-service No 4 had been moved in there in July. Following more rain, the service was suspended after 20 August.

No 4 crosses the Dyfi river bridge with a short goods train. On the far bank of the river, to the left of the train, stone has been tipped to protect against erosion.

No 4 at Maespoeth in 1946.

No 4 with a goods train, including both locomotive coal wagons, in 1947. (G.F. Bannister)

The newly formed Railway Executive then proposed to close the railway between Machynlleth and Aberllefenni, requesting the approval of the British Transport Commission on 29 September 1948. The flooding had caused erosion to within 3in of the rails, it said. Keeping it open would require expenditure of £2,000 to repair the erosion plus £5,400 to renew three other bridges. Revenue in 1947 had been £252 (907 tons) against expenditure of £2,939. The traffic could be worked by road to Machynlleth at an estimated cost of £120 annually. Allowing for some unspecified civil engineering maintenance and renewals required before the closure process was completed there would be a net annual saving of £2,204 if the line was closed. The net cost of recovery of permanent way, equipment and rolling stock was estimated at £1,441.

Regarding the Ratgoed Tramway, worked by 'gravitation and horse', it was the only means of access to the quarries that it served. If the executive continued to work it, annual maintenance and renewals would cost £380 against revenue of £27.

It was proposed to make an arrangement with the quarry owners for them to operate and maintain it until the legal implications of abandonment had been considered, and then to sell it to them if practicable.

The commission approved both the closure and the Ratgoed recommendation when it met on 28 October 1948. Earlier, having read of the railway's closure in the 3 September issue of *Railway Gazette*, the Ministry of Transport had written to ask for confirmation, as it 'might be possible to carry out certain improvements to the trunk road by the use of the railway land'.

J.I.C. Boyd (see bibliography) stated that although demolition was started on 16 November 1948, it was not completed until 1951; track had been lifted between Aberllefenni and Corris when the 1948 Ordnance Survey was made. Ten tons of rail was sold to the Talyllyn Railway in 1949. The river bridge had been demolished by 1953 and a Welsh Government-funded foot/cycle bridge built on its site was opened in 2001.

No 3 at Corris in August 1948. The photographer claimed that this was the penultimate train operated before the railway's closure. Clearly, the weather has started to take its toll on the station roof. (J. Norris/ John Scott Morgan collection)

The damaged embankment, seen on 23 August 1948, just a few days after the railway had been closed. (H.C. Casserley)

Llwyngwern seen at the time of the railway's closure, the quarry's branch already removed.

Llwyngwern c1950.
(David Elliot)

The curve at Pont
Pantperthog, 19 April
1948.

Pont Ifans. (John Scott Morgan collection)

Maespoeth, invaded by sheep,
19 April 1948.

Between the houses at Corris, 1946.

The climb between the fields to Aberllefenni, 19 April 1948. The parapets of one of the railway's overbridges are visible just around the bend.

The Dyfi bridge site with the decking removed, 2 August 1953.

By the 1980s the intermediate bridge piers had either been washed away or removed. April 1984.

The station master at Machynlleth is said to have turned a blind eye to instructions to send the locomotives to Swindon for scrapping – they had been condemned on 25 October 1948 – and kept them covered up until they were sold to the Talyllyn Railway for £25 each, reduced from £85, on 1 March 1951. The TR also bought the eleven remaining wagons for 10s each and was given the surviving brake van purchased by an enthusiast after, allegedly, his wife had refused to allow him to take it home. Parts of the trackbed, including the depot at Maespoeth, were sold to the Forestry Commission in 1955 and Merioneth County Council bought the railway property in Corris.

On 28 March 1952 the Railway Executive asked the British Transport Commission to approve the Ratgoed Tramway's closure. Revenue in 1951 had been £2 11s 4d, of which £1 2s had been for transporting the machinery from the recently closed Ratgoed. The quarry's owner had no further use for the line and did not wish to buy it. There had been no objections to the closure proposals. Annual savings on permanent way repairs were estimated at £30 and recovery of track materials was expected to yield a surplus of £275. Approval to the closure was given on 8 April 1952.

Even without the damaged bridge, the railway would still have been an early candidate for closure. Milne's initial reaction, 'not at any price', was surely the right one for the GWR. It is unlikely to have recouped the railway's minimal purchase price and certainly would not have recouped its expenditure on No 3 authorised in 1929 and the £2,000 spent on the track in 1930. As it was, the railway carried on playing a useful role for the communities and quarries in the Dulas valley, albeit one that was increasingly usurped by road transport, for the best part of another twenty years.

The foot/cycle bridge opened on the site of the railway's Dyfi bridge in 2002.

The locomotives 'in store' at Machynlleth.

On arrival at the Talyllyn Railway,
their new home, 21 April 1951.
(Hugh Ballantyne)

This single bladed point was the junction between the line to Aberllefenni quarry, to the right, and the Ratgoed tramway. A road was later made through this spot. March 1946. (J.I.C. Boyd)

The track from Aberllefenni quarry, looking south.
The slate dressing sheds are on the left. 19 April 1948.

The Ratgoed line crossed the Aberllefenni road, and tramway, by this bridge. The far abutment is still to be seen. (John Scott Morgan collection)

Aberllefenni slate destined for the dressing sheds, the Ratgoed bridge behind. (C.F. Clapper)

With the track removed, the buildings fell into disrepair, albeit they had not been maintained since 1930, at least. Those at Aberllefenni and Corris lasted until the 1960s, the former being taken for a minor road improvement made in connection with the construction of some council houses. Dix's roadside stations at Llwyngwern and Esgairgeiliog had a better future, being taken under the wing of the Corris Railway Society and kept in good order in conjunction with the local authority. The fine Machynlleth headquarters station building has changed hands several times and has been restored, although its modern glazing is out of sympathy with the building.

So far as the slate, the railway's *raison d'être*, is concerned, Braich Goch, the largest quarry, survived until the 1970s. Its tips have been landscaped and part of it opened as a tourist attraction. Gaewern, its neighbour, which had merged with Braich Goch in 1884, closed at the same time. Its open workings are visible from the Abercwmeiddau access road opposite.

Abercwmeiddau itself, abandoned since the 1930s, is overgrown. Aberllefenni lasted until 2003. Attempts to restart quarrying at Ratgoed were abandoned in 1948 but its tips were the source of slab carried to the business established at the former Aberllefenni dressing sheds by the Ratgoed tramway. Llwyngwern has a new life as the Centre for Alternative Technology.

Along the line, the remains of the line to Garreg are slight except for the arch under the standard gauge railway, bricked up in the 1990s. Elsewhere, much of the route parallel to the road is badly overgrown. Road works, widening and realignment, have affected the trackbed at Pantperthog and Pont y Coedwig. In Corris, the bridge over the Deri is largely hidden by falling ivy, and incursions on the trackbed here and road improvements at Garneddwen would prevent the revived railway being restored to Aberllefenni, but the double line of slates set on edge indicate its position through open fields beyond Corris.

From around 1950 the Ratgoed horse was replaced by this tractor, which continued in use until the 1960s. This photograph was taken in the summer of 1962. (Lawrence Wright/Mike Green collection)

Aberllefenni station, 1962. (Lawrence Wright/Mike Green collection)

Although it is imperfect, this 1962 photograph of Corris station gives an impression of the colour used to decorate its woodwork. (Lawrence Wright/Mike Green collection)

This view of the station, from July 1965, shows the original ticket window blocked up and its 1897 replacement accessed from the platform. The building was demolished soon afterwards. (Michael Bishop)

Llwyngwern in 1962, still with its 'warehouse'. (Lawrence Wright/ Mike Green collection)

Seen in 2017, Llwyngwern station building in use as a bus shelter, its office portion demolished after its roof collapsed.

Esgairgeiliog station building as restored by the Corris Railway Society.

The rear of the Machynlleth station building, viewed from a train in 1974.

From the front it can be seen that the building is both neglected and subject to vandalism.

In contrast, its appearance in 2017 is a great improvement, although it has lost most of its chimneys.

Parc Eco Dyfi
Dyfi Eco Park

Gaewern quarry tips and levels, viewed from the Abercwmeiddau quarry access road.

Left: Aberllefenni in 1962. (Lawrence Wright/Mike Green collection)

Middle: A contrasting view of Aberllefenni in 2010.

Right: In the 1990s the Centre for Alternative Technology, based in Llwyngwern quarry, built a water-balanced funicular on the site of the former incline, seen here shortly after it had opened in May 1992.

The arch constructed by the Aberystwyth & Welsh Coast Railway to accommodate the line to Garreg, seen in 1974, called a *latrina* by the vicar of Corris in 1906.

A contrasting view of the arch seen in 2017. It was blocked up by 1982.

The railway bridge over the Deri. Hanging ivy conceals the bridge from the downstream side.

Garneddwen. The railway once crossed the road here, and ran in front of the cottages. Compare with the photograph on page 74.

Abandoned railway formation on the edge of Corris.

CHAPTER 4

REVIVAL

Had it lasted another ten years or so, the Corris Railway would have been a good subject for preservation on closure. As it was, it was 1966 before the Corris Society (Corris Railway Society from 1970) was formed as a study group, with the objective of recording the railway's history and establishing a museum, preferably in the Machynlleth station building.

The notion was not universally welcomed, enthusiast and Talyllyn Railway member Robin Butterell writing to *Railway Magazine* (August 1967) to say that he could not, 'see what valid contribution this can make to the preservation scene, particularly as the locomotives … have been incorporated into the Talyllyn Railway or Narrow Gauge Railway Museum, only a few miles away.'

The society's founders, Alan Lawson and Alan Meaden, replied that the railway had been neglected since its closure and that in their view a local railway could not be divorced from its surroundings, that museum exhibits should include examples of traffic carried to show how transport and industry were linked. 'Exhibits of rolling stock and locomotives are of limited interest,' they continued, 'but when coupled with the effect on life in the neighbourhood the interest is far more general.' They anticipated that the museum would house original relics, models and documents, and forecast that replicas of

The 1896 stable block at Corris, as seen in 1984. The stables were on the lower level, accessed from the rear. The parcels office, the Corris Railway Society's first base, was at the far end, the coach store was accessed by the two large doors, and the tack store was at the right-hand end. Merioneth County Council bought the site from British Railways in the 1960s, demolishing the remains of the station to create a car park just before the society rented the former parcels office in August 1969. Part of the site was then leased to the health authority, which installed two portable buildings for use as a surgery. The site also provides the only access to the village's primary school.

rolling stock could be made and exhibited on suitable track. They would never have dreamed that their efforts would lead to the construction of two steam locomotives and four carriages.

Due to the Machynlleth building's unavailability, the former parcels office in Corris was rented from 20 August 1969 and the museum established in it subsequently expanded into the former coach store. With a wagon displayed on a short length of track outside in 1971, the building was purchased from Dolgellau Rural District Council for £150 in 1972.

A change in emphasis towards developing an operating railway rather than just a museum attracted more interest and led to the registration of the

Corris Railway Company Ltd in 1976 and the registration of the society as an educational charity in 1977. Advised that a Light Railway Order would be required before rides could be offered to members of the public, the company settled on the notion of restoring the railway between Corris and Llwyngwern, 3¼ miles, and operating in conjunction with the Centre for Alternative Technology, which had been established in Llwyngwern quarry. Negotiations with the Welsh Office, which was to take some of the trackbed for road improvements, were protracted.

A length of demonstration track had been laid at Corris in 1976 and more progress followed the employment of five

The rear of the stable building, showing the stable entrance. Dix's problematical dung heap would have been somewhere nearby; the river is behind the photographer. The railway bought the land on the right in 2019.

The society's museum, in the former coach house, as seen in 1992. Arranged along the far wall are the remains of the second carriage that finished up in Gobowen.

The external display established in 1971.

men funded by the Manpower Services Commission in 1978. They restored boundary walls, installed drains and worked on the old stable block.

Fulfilment of the society's ambitions has been a long process. Plans for reviving the railway with a 2½ mile line from Corris to the Forestry Commission picnic site at Tan y Coed, near Esgairgeiliog, were first drawn up in 1981. A planning application to reinstate the railway in 1984 was declared void on the basis of a technicality and was only accepted by Gwynedd County Council following Welsh Office intervention two years later. A further intervention was required after another two years, when two sub-committees had recommended approval but the full council resolved not to make a decision, which was not an option under planning law.

Following further prevarication, in 1992 the council formally refused planning permission, but faced with the railway's determination to appeal, backed down, asking for a fresh application which it approved in January 1994. By this time the railway had missed the boat for its intended Light Railway Order application, for the legislation had been repealed and replaced by the Transport & Works Act, an altogether much more complex and expensive procedure, in 1992. Later, the council's change in strategy was confirmed by the reservation of the trackbed for railway purposes in the Eryri Local District Plan.

Meanwhile, the former loco shed at Maespoeth had been bought from the Forestry Commission with the aid of a £1,350 grant from the Development Board for Rural Wales in 1981 and track laying between Corris and Maespoeth had been completed in 1985. Additional land on the opposite side of the track to the shed was purchased in 1998 and a two-road carriage shed built there, mostly by volunteers, in 2007/8. Capable of accommodating eight carriages and two vans, it is equipped with a small work area and an inspection pit.

The Forestry Commission bought the land and loco shed at Maespoeth from British Railways, establishing a depot to process cut timber. This was the scene in 1955. (Robert Darlaston)

By July 1963 the stable door had been blocked up.

The same scene in 1984, three years after the society had moved in.

A works train between Maespoeth and Corris in June 1992. The carriage is an ex-colliery manrider loaned by the Centre for Alternative Technology.

A member paid for the materials for a new carriage. Built on a wagon underframe, the result is a miniature version of the original bogie carriages. 26 June 1992.

Maespoeth on 11 April 2009, with the carriage shed nearing completion.

Following an inspection on 15 March 2002, a minor relaxation of the rules permitted the start of passenger services between Corris and Maespoeth on 3 June, but a Transport & Works Order will be required before there can be any extension involving public level crossings. As well as dealing with the railway inspectorate, the society also had to deal with the various successors to British Rail, because they held the railway operating rights in succession to British Railways. Operating on 28 days before closing for the winter, 1,393 passengers were carried in 2002.

The official opening was performed by Christopher Awdry, son of the creator of *Thomas the Tank Engine*, on 7 June 2003, although he was outshone by the operation of ex-Corris Railway Hughes 0-4-2ST No 3, passenger carriage and van courtesy of the Talyllyn Railway. The inaugural train was waved away by a guard carrying the silver fusee watch presented to Edward Thomas, a predecessor, to commemorate his retirement after thirty years' employment in 1896. Thomas had been one of those prosecuted for taking wagons on the road in 1886/7.

The first steam operation on the revived railway had occurred in October 1996 to help launch the railway's own new-build steam locomotive project, the Talyllyn Railway lending a Corris Railway goods train, comprising Kerr, Stuart 'Tattoo' 0-4-2ST No 4, the van and several wagons for ten days. With public operation over two weekends and a photographic train, the event attracted good publicity and crowds.

Knowing that steam operation would be more attractive to visitors, but with the railway's gauge restricting the options available, the scheme for the new locomotive had been announced in 1995. Paid for mostly by supporters making donations by subscription, the locomotive was delivered in May 2005, its first day in service on 20 August. No 7 in the railway's fleet, it had cost £130,000. In 2009, the railway announced that it would build a second new locomotive, a new Hughes 0-4-2ST, funded in the

same manner. Estimated to cost £250,000, construction was started in 2011 and is making good progress at the time of publication.

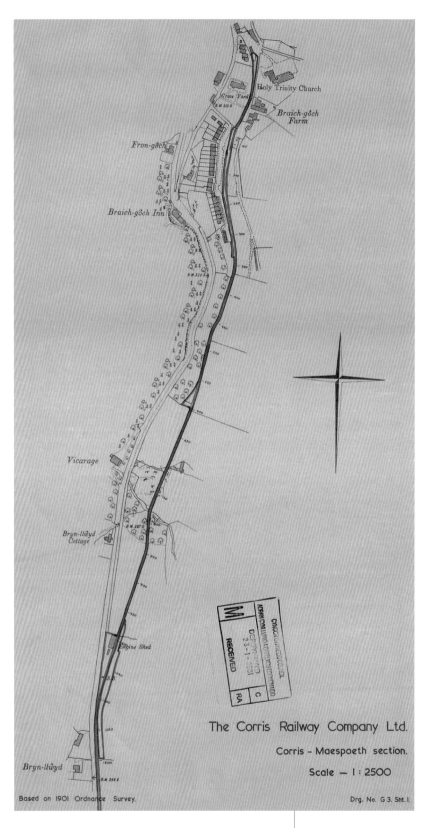

The Corris Railway Company Ltd.

Corris – Maespoeth section.

Scale — 1 : 2500

Based on 1901 Ordnance Survey.

Drg. No. G 3. Sht.I.

The plan that accompanied the 2001 planning application for the new carriage shed.

Accommodation on the first passenger train on 3 June 2002 comprised the four-wheeled carriage and a van.

Chris Awdry (left) and society chairman Keith Davies, and the plaque unveiled by the former on 7 June 2003, commemorating the railway's reopening.

The Corris Railway train loaned by the Talyllyn Railway, approaching Corris on 7 June 2003.

Corris station on 7 June 2003. The surgery is on the right.

Courtesy of the Talyllyn Railway, a Corris Railway goods train approaches the village on 24 October 1996.

The same formation leaving Corris on 18 October 1996.

On 7 October 2003 society members visited the works of Winson Engineering in Daventry, Northamptonshire, to view the rolling chassis of their new locomotive.

The finished product, No 7 in the railway's stock list, in steam at Maespoeth on 30 May 2005.

No 7 inside
Maespoeth shed on
30 May 2016.

No 7 leaves the shed
ready to start work.
The gantry erected
over the Upper
Corris tramway is
used for loading and
unloading equipment
and materials.

The boiler for Hughes 0-4-2ST No 10 on display in the carriage shed to encourage support for the new loco.

No 7 passes Maespoeth signal box, a recreation of the original structure. Unlike the original railway, which used vacuum brakes, the revival uses air brakes.

A headboard commemorating the railway's 150th anniversary was carried by No 7 on 11 April 2009.

Owner Ian Cryer and his horse Truman demonstrate animal haulage of wagons at Maespoeth on 11 April 2009.

No 21, the first of four full size bogie carriages, entered service in 2009.

Carriage No 22, seen on 30 May 2016, has a clerestory roof.

Carriage No 22's worksplate. No 21 was built in a member's workshop in Nottingham.

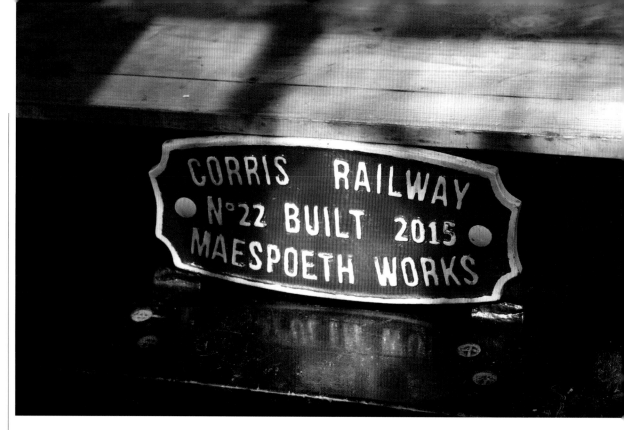

Carriage No 23 under construction in the carriage shed. The original vehicles did not have the steel body frames shown here.

The railway received a lot of publicity when No 7 and carriage No 22 attended the Warley Model Railway Show held at the National Exhibition Centre in November 2013.

No 7 poses with a rake of original Corris Railway vehicles during a visit to the Talyllyn Railway in October 2011. Driver Mike Green, who was passed to drive on both railways, has charge of the loco.

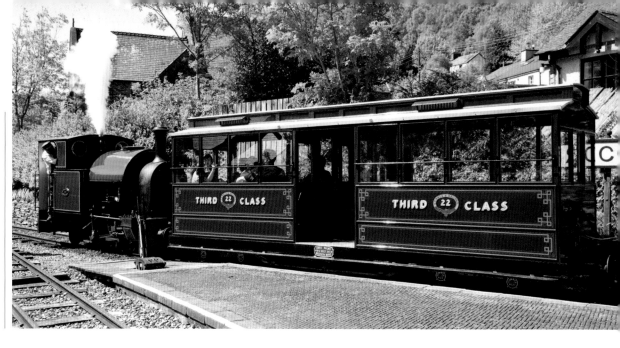

Until the surgery site at Corris was acquired trains were propelled to the village and pulled back to Maespoeth. 30 May 2016.

The plan submitted by the railway company in support of its application to develop the station area in 2010.

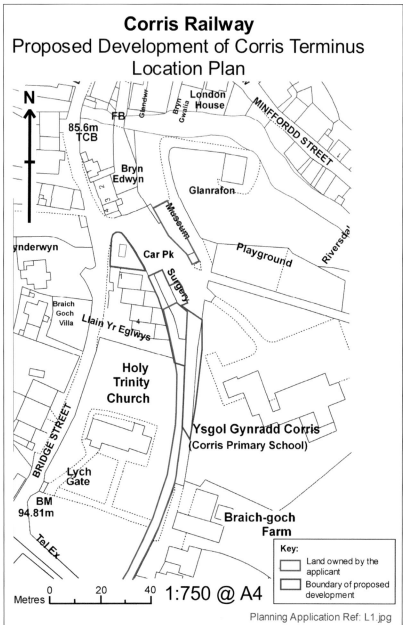

Corris Railway
Proposed Development of Corris Terminus
Location Plan

N

85.6m
TCB

FB

London
House

Glandwr

Bryn
Gwalia

MINFFORDD STREET

Bryn
Edwyn

Glanrafon

Museum

Playground

Riversdal

ynderwyn

Car Pk

Surgery

Braich
Goch
Villa

Llain Yr Eglwys

Holy
Trinity
Church

BRIDGE STREET

Lych
Gate

Ysgol Gynradd Corris
(Corris Primary School)

BM
94.81m

Tal Ex

Braich-goch
Farm

Key:
☐ Land owned by the applicant
☐ Boundary of proposed development

Metres 0 20 40 1:750 @ A4

Planning Application Ref: L1.jpg

The railway's 150th anniversary was celebrated with aplomb in 2009, with trains hauled by its own steam locomotive and including the first of four new bogie carriages. Built to a design that J.R. Dix would have recognised, this one was built in a member's workshop in Nottingham, the others in the new shed at Maespoeth. A member paid for the materials, volunteers donated their time and labour to construct them.

Closure of the surgery located in portable buildings on part of the original station site at Corris enabled the land to be purchased in 2016 and the running line and platform extended. Plans for a new station on the site, complete with an overall roof, had been drawn up in 2010, when the society had expected to pay for the surgery to be relocated. Planning permission was given in October 2011. Now, unhampered by the need to accommodate the health centre, in 2016 members were encouraged to raise £47,000 to pay for a new turn-out and traverser to enable trains to be hauled in both directions.

Changes to rules, procedures and authorities since the railway's revival was first mooted, has meant that planning and implementation of an 800m deviation at Pont y Coedwig has been protracted, increasing costs considerably. Work on the ground was started in 2011. In 2017 the society announced that when the deviation is completed services will be extended to Pont Ifans as a first stage towards extending to Tyn y Coed.

The running line extension at Corris, made possible after the surgery had been vacated and the site purchased by the railway. 30 May 2016.

A train and its crew wait for time in the enlarged station, 10 June 2018.

The prospect of being able to run round trains at Corris leads to the construction of a new platform and a run-round loop to the south of the loco shed at Maespoeth. The water crane was made to the railway's specification at the Brunswick Ironworks in Caernarfon. 10 June 2018.

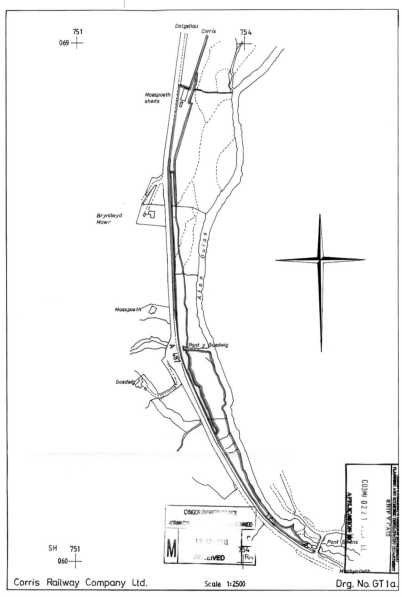

The last two Corris Railway locomotives remain popular additions to the Talyllyn Railway fleet, joined by a brake van and eleven wagons sold by BR. In 1958 the TR also acquired one of the carriage bodies sold by the GWR in 1930 from a Gobowen garden, restoring it to service in 1961. The remains of the second were retrieved in 1968 and are on display in the railway's museum.

A link with the past was broken when Gwilym Evan Jones died in June 1998, aged 94, the last known surviving Corris Railway Company employee; he had been a porter and guard. When the GWR took over in 1930 he was transferred to Oswestry, remaining a railwayman until he retired.

The Corris Railway has faced obstacles unknown to any other railway since it was founded, overcoming them by sheer determination. The same determination will take it forward to fulfil its dreams and objectives.

The planning application plan for the Coedwig deviation, submitted in 2013.

Looking south on 16 December 2016, where the Coedwig deviation will join the original formation.

Pont Ifans, proposed to be an intermediate terminus as the railway extends southwards. A Transport & Works Order will be required before it can go further.

Both original Corris Railway locomotives, and a glimpse of the Corris carriage, at the Talyllyn Railway on 16 October 2011.

The Talyllyn Railway's Corris Railway carriage, recovered from a garden in Gobowen, shortly after it had been restored to service on 22 May 1961.

Probably the most famous person to travel in a Corris Railway carriage did so on the Talyllyn Railway on 25 November 1983. The TR rostered its Corris carriage in the train that ran between Pendre and Rhydyronen for TRH the Prince and Princess of Wales. While her husband rode on the loco, Princess Diana travelled in the carriage, seen here passing Hendy. (G.F. Bannister)

The Museum in 2017. Some panels have been added to the remains of carriage No 7 to demonstrate its construction and purpose.

A view of the station area and its surroundings as seen from the cemetery, 21 February 2018. The stable block was in the process of being re-roofed.

CORRIS RAILWAY

An enamel poster board header displayed in the Narrow Gauge Railway Museum at Tywyn.

ACTS OF PARLIAMENT

1852   Corris, Machynlleth and River Dovey Railway
1858   Corris, Machynlleth and River Dovey Tramroad
1864   Corris Railway
1880   Corris Railway
1883   Corris Railway

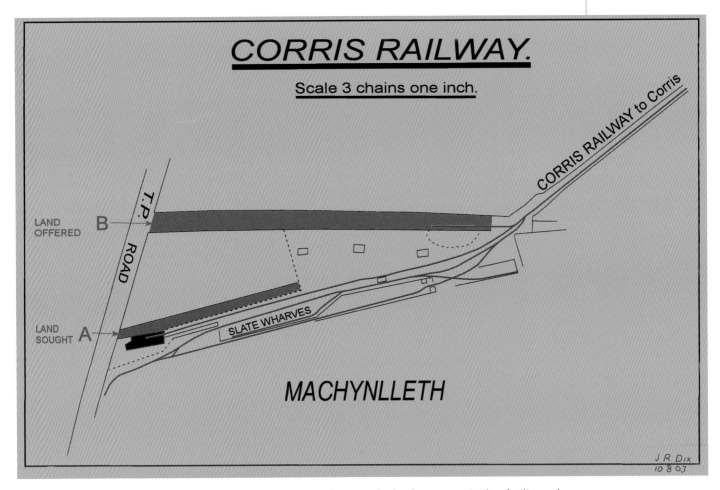

Produced in August 1903, Dix's plan of Machynlleth station showing the land swap required to facilitate the construction of the new station building was not the finest example of the draughtman's art; this illustration is a tracing of it. (National Archives)

LOCOMOTIVES

No 1 Hughes 0-4-0ST (324/1878), 0-4-2ST c1886, rebuilt 1895, not used after 1921

No 2 Hughes 0-4-0ST (322/1878), 0-4-2ST c1886, rebuilt 1898, stored serviceable 1921-4. Out of use by 1925.

No 3 Hughes 0-4-0ST (323/1878), 0-4-2ST c1886, rebuilt 1900, condemned 25 October 1948, sold to Talyllyn Railway 1 March 1951; recorded mileage when sold – 64,341

No 4 Kerr, Stuart 'Tattoo' 0-4-2ST (4047/1921); number allocated by GWR, condemned 25 October 1948, sold to Talyllyn Railway 1 March 1951; recorded mileage when sold – 198,566

No 5 Motor Rail 4wDM (22258/1965) *Alan Meaden*, acquired 1974, restored 1980

No 6 Ruston Hornsby 4wDH (518493/1966), acquired 1982, restored 1996

No 7 Kerr, Stuart 'Tattoo' 0-4-2ST (Winson Engineering/Drayton Designs 17/2005)

No 8 Hunslet 4wDM (7274/1973), on loan from National Mining Museum 2002

No 9 Clayton Engineering 4wBE (B0457/1974) *Aberllefenni*, acquired 2007

No 10 Hughes 0-4-2ST

Not taken into GWR stock, Nos 1 and 2 were scrapped by Peter Vaughan & Son of Machynlleth in 1930.

No 10 is under construction at the time of publication.

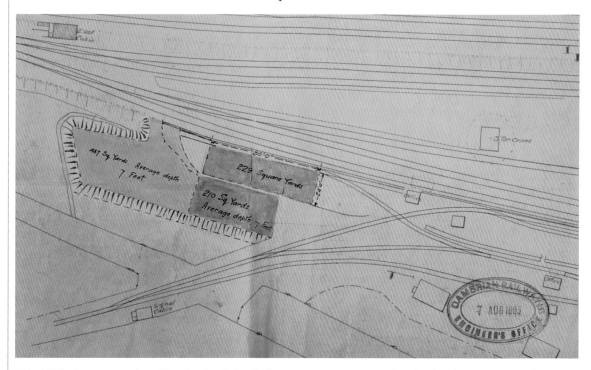

This 1905 plan was produced by the Cambrian Railways to support an application by the proprietor of Maglona Quarries Ltd, operators of Llwyngwern, producer of slate slabs for billiard tables and mantle pieces, to increase the area of land leased from that company at Machynlleth to provide more stacking space adjacent to the existing wharf. Served only by the Corris Railway, the land already occupied by the quarry is coloured blue and red, the additional land coloured green. (National Archives)

BOARD OF TRADE RETURNS

	1872	1873	1874	1875	1876	1877	1878	1879	1882	1883	1880	1881
Authorised capital												
Shares/stock	£15,000	£15,000	£15,000	£15,000	£15,000	£15,000	£15,000	£15,000	£15,000	£15,000	£15,000	£15,000
Loans/debentures	£5,000	£5,000	£5,000	£5,000	£5,000	£5,000	£5,000	£5,000	£5,000	£5,000	£5,000	£5,000
Issued												
5% debentures	£4,250	£4,300	£4,800	£4,950	£4,950	£4,950	£4,950	£4,950	£4,950	£4,950	£4,950	£4,950
Dividend	5.75%	4.50%	4.50%	4.75%	7.25%	8.50%	6.50%		1.13%	4.38%		2.25%
Passengers carried												
First class										764		
Third class		in open trucks	3,592	11,830	16,169	18,433	22,024	3,232		19,398		
Total			3,592	11,830	16,169	18,433	22,024	3,232		20,162		
Goods, mineral and livestock traffic												
Merchandise (tons)						818	900	817	1,795	2,102	1,474	1,700
Minerals (tons)	15,669	15,694	14,532	16,461	18,681	19,918	16,195	13,209	15,234	17,836	16,247	15,843
Train miles												
Passenger										5,345		
Goods									7,178	7,824		3,800
Total										13,169		
Revenue receipts												
Passengers												
First class										£30		
Third class			£90	£290	£372	£414	£523	£74		£387		
Total receipts from passengers			£90	£290	£372	£414	£523	£74		£417		
Mails and parcel post										£7		
Goods train traffic												
Merchandise						£157	£198	£235	£320	£365	£310	£343
Minerals	£1,648	£1,594	£1,512	£1,726	£1,816	£1,818	£1,467	£1,225	£1,563	£1,845	£1,561	£1,516
Total goods train receipts	£1,648	£1,594	£1,512	£1,726	£1,816	£1,975	£1,665	£1,460	£1,883	£2,210	£1,871	£1,859
Miscellaneous								£262	£3	£3	£5	£4
Traffic revenue	£1,648	£1,594	£1,602	£3,742	£2,188	£2,389	£2,188	£1,796	£1,886	£2,657	£1,876	£1,863
Revenue expenditure												
Maintenance of way and works	£381	£529	£373	£467	£391	£424	£381	£343	£285	£304	£236	£273
Maintenance of rolling stock	£117	£107	£183	£212	£44	£31	£24	£40		£44	£6	£24

	1872	1873	1874	1875	1876	1877	1878	1879	1882	1883	1880	1881
Loco running expenses (Hire of horses)	£31	£8	£113	£275	£260	£265	£342	£403	£166	£208	£462	£158
Traffic expenses									£460	£794		£300
General charges	£104	£111	£109	£82	£101	£78	£89	£571	£352	£171	£415	£373
Rents and rates	£29	£30	£31	£14	£27	£17	£23	£37	£91	£66	£64	£45
Government duty			£4	£14	£17	£21	£26	£4		£2		
Damage and loss of goods, property, &c									£1	£1	£4	£21
Legal and Parliamentary						£8	£6	£69	£35	£21	£274	£73
Miscellaneous									£51	£4	£77	£22	£71
Total expenditure	£662	£785	£813	£1,064	£840	£844	£891	£1,518	£1,394	£1,688	£1,483	£1,338
Total receipts	£1,648	£1,594	£1,602	£2,016	£2,188	£2,389	£2,188	£1,796	£1,886	£2,657	£1,876	£1,863
Net receipts	£986	£809	£789	£952	£1,348	£1,545	£1,297	£278	£492	£949	£393	£525
Ratio expenditure/ receipts	40%	40%	51%	53%	38%	35%	41%	85%	74%	64%	79%	72%
Rolling stock												
Steam locomotives									3	3	3	3
Passenger carriages								10	10	10	10	10
Merchandise and mineral vehicles	'Haulage done by horses. The company has only a few slate trucks.'							13	12	12	11	11
Any other carriages or wagons not listed									1			2

	1882	1883	1884	1885	1886	1887	1888	1889	1890	1891
Authorised capital										
Shares/stock	£15,000	£15,000	£15,000	£15,000	£15,000	£15,000	£15,000	£15,000	£15,000	£15,000
Loans/debentures	£5,000	£5,000	£5,000	£5,000	£5,000	£5,000	£5,000	£5,000	£5,000	£5,000
Issued										
5% debentures	£4,950	£4,950	£4,950	£4,950	£4,950	£4,950	£4,950	£4,950	£4,950	£4,950
Capital expenditure				£19,944	£19,929	£19,918	£19,898	£19,970	£19,989	£19,995
During year				£6						
Dividend	1.13%	4.38%	4.38%	5%	2.25%	3%	3%	2.00%		1.88%
Passengers carried										
First class		764	2,628	2,540	2,032	2,638	2,224	2,381	2,562	2,281
Third class		19,398	44,993	48,922	45,812	46,586	54,178	55,149	58,302	58,482
Total		20,162	47,621	51,462	47,844	49,224	56,402	57,530	60,864	60,763
Season tickets			262	737	1,630	1,638	1,800	334	766	1,037
Goods, mineral and livestock traffic										
Merchandise (tons)	1,795	2,102	2,167	2,290	1,959	1,870	2,280	1,862	2,253	2,510
Minerals (tons)	15,234	17,836	16,834	17,297	16,444	16,756	17,431	15,218	14,600	13,546
Train miles										
Passenger		5,345	11,725	11,490	10,755	12,285	13,515	13,190	13,223	12,960
Goods	7,178	7,824	8,720	8,562	6,260	8,389	9,811	9,118	4,636	9,561

	1882	1883	1884	1885	1886	1887	1888	1889	1890	1891
Total		13,169	20,445	20,052	17,015	20,674	23,326	22,308	17,859	22,521
Revenue receipts										
Passengers										
First class		£30	£93	£88	£68	£87	£73	£76	£86	£85
Third class		£387	£822	£853	£761	£760	£845	£863	£920	£913
Season tickets			£10	£50	£96	£96	£105	£15	£52	£60
Total receipts from passengers		£417	£925	£991	£925	£943	£1,023	£954	£1,058	£1,058
Parcels under 2cwt and excess luggage				£13	£9	£10	£14	£15	£48	£87
Mails and parcel post		£7	£40	£40	£40	£40	£50	£50	£50	£50
Total passenger train receipts		£424	£965	£1,044	£974	£993	£1,087	£1,019	£1,156	£1,195
Goods train traffic										
Merchandise	£320	£365	£388	£444	£408	£390	£467	£399	£386	£384
Minerals	£1,563	£1,845	£1,719	£1,839	£1,637	£1,690	£1,727	£1,526	£1,462	£1,439
Total goods train receipts	£1,883	£2,210	£2,107	£2,283	£2,045	£2,080	£2,194	£1,925	£1,848	£1,823
Talyllyn coaches									£106	£96
Posting									£19	£42
Miscellaneous	£3	£3	£4	£6	£4	£6	£6	£124	£14	£156
Traffic revenue	£1,886	£2,657	£3,076	£3,333	£3,023	£3,079	£3,287	£3,068	£3,026	£3,174
Revenue expenditure										
Maintenance of way and works	£285	£304	£477	£614	£799	£561	£682	£533	£375	£512
Maintenance of rolling stock		£44	£21	£45	£36	£21	£180	£237	£242	£173
Loco running expenses (Hire of horses)	£166	£208	£294	£312	£279	£406	£301	£311	£342	£456
Traffic expenses	£460	£794	£872	£1,055	£1,020	£1,091	£1,131	£1,148	£564	£1,186
General charges	£352	£171	£343	£193	£196	£223	£181	£199	£198	£190
Rents and rates	£91	£66	£78	£83	£57	£80	£93	£64	£67	£82
Government duty		£2	£9	£11	£10	£11	£13	£14	£14	£14
Damage and loss of goods, property, &c	£1	£1	£16		£2	£4				
Legal and Parliamentary	£35	£21	£20	£25						
Miscellaneous	£4	£77								
Total expenditure	£1,394	£1,688	£2,130	£2,338	£2,399	£2,397	£2,581	£2,506	£1,802	£2,613
Total receipts	£1,886	£2,657	£3,076	£3,333	£3,023	£3,079	£3,287	£3,068	£3,026	£3,174
Net receipts	£492	£949	£946	£995	£624	£682	£706	£562	£1,224	£561
Ratio expenditure/receipts	74%	64%	69%	70%	79%	78%	79%	82%	75%	82%
Rolling stock										
Steam locomotives	3	3	3	3	3	3	3	3	3	3
Passenger carriages	10	10	10	10	10	10	11	10	9	8
Other coaching vehicles				1	1	1	1	1	1	1
Merchandise and mineral vehicles	11	11	11	13	14	14	15	15	18	18
Any other carriages or wagons not listed	1									

	1882	1883	1884	1885	1886	1887	1888	1889	1890	1891
Goods and parcels road vehicles										
Posting									279	601
									37	138
Total									316	739
Total									£19	£42
Talyllyn coaches										
									2,240	1,989
									£106	£96
Coaching stock										
Composite 1st/3rd									1	1
3rd								2	2	3
4w 1st			4	4	4	4	2	2	2	2
4w 3rd			6	6	6	6	9	6	4	2
Brake Van			1	1	1	1	1	1	1	1
Large iron wagons			9	9	9	9	9	6	6	6
Small iron wagons								3	3	3
Wooden wagons			2	4	5	5	5	6	7	7
Timber trucks									2	2
Directors' fees				40	80	80	80	80	80	80
Salaries					80	80	80	80	80	80

	1892	1893	1894	1895	1896	1897	1898	1899	1900	1901
Authorised capital										
Shares/stock	£15,000	£15,000	£15,000	£15,000	£15,000	£15,000	£15,000	£15,000	£15,000	£15,000
Loans/debentures	£5,000	£5,000	£5,000	£5,000	£5,000	£5,000	£5,000	£5,000	£5,000	£5,000
Issued										
5% debentures	£4,950	£4,950	£4,950	£4,950	£5,000	£5,000	£5,000	£5,000	£5,000	£5,000
Capital expenditure	£20,044	£20,199	£20,305	£20,262	£20,605	£20,690	£21,177	£21,166	£21,113	£21,203
During year						£122				£90
Dividend	1.88%	6.50%	6.75%	5.50%	6.25%	6.00%	5.00%	6.00%	6.00%	5.00%
Passengers carried										
First class	2,203	2,408	1,998	1,565	1,450	1,697	1,870	1,571	1,552	1,497
Third class	56,619	62,906	68,373	78,236	74,757	77,344	81,174	80,859	76,510	72,991
Total	58,822	65,314	70,371	79,801	76,207	79,041	83,044	82,430	78,062	74,488
Workmen's tickets										
Season tickets	1,521	2,165	2,973	2,092	1,590	3,509	5,202	4,843	4,302	3,136
Goods, mineral and livestock traffic										
Merchandise (tons)	2,384	2,636	2,632	2,611	2,424	2,661	2,772	2,971	3,100	2,603
Minerals (tons)	16,369	17,608	17,145	16,480	16,048	17,027	16,965	16,613	17,724	17,663
Train miles										
Passenger	13,075	13,403	13,555	13,665	13,725	14,300	14,310	14,545	14,570	14,476

	1892	1893	1894	1895	1896	1897	1898	1899	1900	1901
Goods	10,914	10,877	10,883	11,379	11,113	11,224	11,512	10,601	10,083	10,444
Total	23,989	24,280	24,438	25,044	24,838	25,524	25,822	25,146	24,653	24,920
Revenue receipts										
Passengers										
First class	£78	£84	£70	£54	£52	£57	£62	£50	£50	£49
Third class	£880	£949	£1,265	£1,070	£1,139	£1,155	£1,159	£1,151	£1,073	£1,053
Season tickets	£76	£123	£155	£139	£87	£181	£297	£231	£208	£150
Total receipts from passengers	£1,034	£1,156	£1,490	£1,263	£1,278	£1,393	£1,518	£1,432	£1,331	£1,252
Parcels under 2cwt and excess luggage	£80	£80	£80	£103	£109	£110	£113	£124	£124	£121
Mails and parcel post	£50	£50	£50	£50	£50	£50	£50	£50	£50	£52
Total passenger train receipts	£1,164	£1,286	£1,620	£1,416	£1,437	£1,553	£1,681	£1,606	£1,505	£1,425
Goods train traffic										
Merchandise	£379	£377	£393	£399	£387	£416	£451	£445	£445	£390
Minerals	£1,893	£2,020	£1,958	£1,886	£1,839	£1,915	£1,791	£1,819	£1,916	£1,913
Total goods train receipts	£2,272	£2,397	£2,351	£2,285	£2,226	£2,331	£2,242	£2,264	£2,361	£2,303
Talyllyn coaches	£131	£168	£223	£293	£113	£273		£368	£383	£388
Posting	£23	£25	£26	£24	£222	£48		£56	£53	£45
Miscellaneous	£172	£221	£24	£344	£364	£35	£367	£16	£23	£23
Traffic revenue	£3,608	£3,904	£3,995	£4,045	£4,027	£3,919	£4,290	£4,310	£4,325	£4,184
Maintenance of way and works	£636	£495	£588	£608	£457	£857	£693	£413	£420	£508
Maintenance of rolling stock	£270	£201	£87	£77	£114	£78	£169	£237	£136	£44
Loco running expenses	£602	£435	£435	£559	£522	£382	£625	£472	£638	£630
Traffic expenses	£1,218	£1,244	£1,288	£1,372	£1,386	£1,340	£1,363	£1,266	£1,300	£1,444
General charges	£19	£199	£205	£193	£196	£300	£331	£441	£431	£346
Rents and rates	£88	£93	£105	£79	£70	£96	£65	£83	£97	£73
Government duty	£14	£14	£13	£13	£13	£13	£17	£15	£14	£13
Damage and loss of goods, property, &c		£12		£15		£16				
Legal and Parliamentary								£205	£69	
Miscellaneous				£51	£38					£55
Total expenditure	£2,847	£2,693	£2,721	£2,967	£2,796	£3,082	£3,263	£3,132	£3,105	£3,113
Total receipts	£3,608	£3,904	£3,995	£4,045	£4,027	£3,919	£4,290	£4,310	£4,325	£4,184
Net receipts	£761	£1,211	£1,274	£1,078	£1,231	£837	£1,027	£1,178	£1,220	£1,071
Ratio expenditure/receipts	79%	69%	68%	73%	69%	79%	76%	73%	72%	74%
Rolling stock										
Steam locomotives	3	3	3	3	3	3	3	3	3	3
Passenger carriages	7	6	6	6	6	8	8	8	8	8
Other coaching vehicles	1	1	1	1	1	1	1	1	1	1
Merchandise and mineral vehicles	18	18	18	18	18	18	18	18	18	18
Posting	333	276	314	384	438	456				
	46	152	95	78	395	395				
Total	379	428	409	462	833	851	1,050	1,019	1,068	691

	1892	1893	1894	1895	1896	1897	1898	1899	1900	1901
	£20	£17	£21	£20	£34	£27				
	£3	£8	£5	£4	£18	£21				
Total	£23	£25	£26	£24	£52	£48	£51	£56	£53	£44
Talyllyn coaches	366	421	382	621	669	659				
	2,176	3,026	4,351	5,760	4,196	5,449				
Total	2,542	3,447	4,733	6,381	4,865	6,108	6,205	8,158	8,021	8,450
	£18	£23	£19	£29	£34	£197				
	£113	£145	£204	£264	£79	£242				
Total	£131	£168	£223	£293	£113	£439	£290	£368	£383	£398
Coaching stock										
Composite 1st/3rd	2	2	2	2	2	2	3	3	3	3
3rd	3	4	4	4	4	4	5	5	5	5
4w 1st	1									
4w 3rd	1									
Brake Van	1	1	1	1	1	1	1	1	1	1
Large iron wagons	6	6	6	6	6	6	6	6	6	6
Small iron wagons	3	3	3	3	3	3	3	3	3	3
Wooden wagons	7	7	7	7	7	7	7	7	7	7
Timber trucks	2	2	2	2	2	2	2	2	2	2
Directors' fees	80	80	80	80	80	80	80	80	80	80
Salaries	80	80	80	80	80	180	180	280	280	280

Notwithstanding the caption, this is a view of Pont Ifans looking towards Maespoeth. Some work is taking place on the Machynlleth side of the crossing and one of the railway's three trolleys is leaning against the wall.

	1902	1903	1904	1905	1906	1907	1908	1909	1910	1911	1912	1913	1914	1915
Authorised capital														
Shares/stock	£15,000	£15,000	£15,000	£15,000	£15,000	£15,000	£15,000	£15,000	£15,000	£15,000	£15,000	£15,000	£15,000	£15,000
Loans/debentures	£5,000	£5,000	£5,000	£5,000	£5,000	£5,000	£5,000	£5,000	£5,000	£5,000	£5,000	£5,000	£5,000	£5,000
Issued														
5% debentures	£5,000	£5,000	£5,000	£5,000	£5,000	£5,000	£5,000	£5,000	£5,000	£5,000	£5,000	£5,000	£5,000	£5,000
Capital expenditure	£21,262	£21,223	£21,272	£21,307	£21,323	£21,208	£23,283	£23,256	£23,256	£23,229	£23,201	£23,174	£23,120	£23,120
Dividend	6.00%	6.00%	4.00%	1.00%										
Passengers carried														
First class	1,506	1,573	1,656	1,595	1,384	1,193	2,419	2,196	2,354	2,256	2,322	2,496		2,507
Third class	72,944	68,838	70,975	62,803	57,019	52,969	57,997	51,165	47,113	48,287	44,577	46,256		35,722
Total	74,450	70,411	72,631	64,398	58,403	54,162	60,416	53,361	49,467	50,543	46,899	48,752		38,229
Workmen's tickets												1,523		1,008
Season tickets	63	46	50	27	14	20	22	20	11	9	6	6		8
Goods, mineral and livestock traffic														
Merchandise (tons)	2,919	2,668	3,088	2,666	2,613	2,356	1,842	1,508	2,328	2,524	2,528	1,139		2,125
Coal, coke and patent fuel (tons)												722		704
Minerals (tons)	18,550	16,741	13,980	10,585	9,196	6,318	6,495	6,178	6,059	6,223	5,892	6,980		4,668
Train miles														
Passenger	14,565	14,488	15,471	14,840	13,900	16,199	25,718	25,001	23,385	23,305	19,910			
Goods	10,564	10,333	9,894	7,819	7,100	7,300	3,222	3,402	3,369	3,606	2,430			
Other												20,751		17,540
Total	25,129	24,821	25,365	22,659	21,000	23,499	28,940	28,403	26,754	26,911	22,340	20,751		17,540
Revenue receipts														
Passengers														
First class	£49	£53	£57	£57	£48	£38	£62	£55	£60	£58	£55	£63		£65
Second class														
Third class	£1,049	£1,009	£996	£899	£817	£797	£798	£701	£719	£759	£740	£788		£609
Season tickets	£163	£110	£134	£71	£36	£53	£57	£53	£30	£33	£24	£3		£8
Workmen's tickets												£11		£7
Total receipts from passengers	£1,261	£1,172	£1,187	£1,027	£901	£888	£917	£809	£809	£850	£819	£865		£689
Parcels under 2cwt and excess luggage	£122	£118	£120	£119	£123	£114	£112	£107	£104	£113	£122	£130		£129
Mails and parcel post	£55	£41	£69	£55	£55	£55	£55	£55	£55	£55	£55	£55		£55
Total passenger train receipts	£1,438	£1,331	£1,376	£1,201	£1,079	£1,057	£1,084	£971	£968	£1,018	£996	£1,050		£873
Goods train traffic														
Merchandise	£432	£382	£419	£377	£392	£347	£319	£236	£367	£414	£347	£115		£380

	1902	1903	1904	1905	1906	1907	1908	1909	1910	1911	1912	1913	1914	1915
Coal, coke, etc												£83		£81
Minerals	£2,019	£1,857	£1,536	£1,192	£1,070	£753	£742	£757	£767	£789	£743	£632		£572
Total goods train receipts	£2,451	£2,239	£1,955	£1,569	£1,462	£1,100	£1,061	£993	£1,134	£1,203	£1,090	£830		£1,033
Talyllyn coaches									£205					
Posting									£43					
Miscellaneous	£492	£430	£469	£460	£490	£351	£340	£294	£9	£527	£713	£29		£16
Traffic revenue	£4,381	£4,000	£3,800	£3,230	£3,031	£2,508	£2,485	£2,258	£2,200	£2,748	£2,799	£1,909		£1,648
Revenue expenditure														
Maintenance of way and works	£554	£462	£461	£506	£511	£304	£312	£320	£340	£326	£315	£397		£318
Maintenance of rolling stock	£68	£103	£66	£54	£43	£19	£60	£87	£60	£143	£54	£140		£233
Loco running expenses (Hire of horses)	£577	£263	£481	£466	£402	£387	£414	£507	£399	£404	£426	£307		£295
Traffic expenses	£1,556	£1,382	£1,352	£1,295	£1,281	£1,282	£1,179	£1,082	£1,135	£1,393	£1,483	£750		£569
General charges	£346	£364	£364	£364	£365	£305	£311	£321	£263	£285	£291	£304		£278
Rents and rates	£83	£76	£75	£69	£96	£114	£83	£87	£97	£106	£97	£75		£95
Government duty	£12	£13	£13	£12	£9	£8	£16	£14	£14	£15	£15	£16		£14
Compensation - personal injury						£2								
Damage and loss of goods, property, &c				£6		£5								
Legal and Parliamentary		£130	£75					£50						
National insurance											£8	£42		£15
Miscellaneous	£54	£48	£45	£46	£23									
Total expenditure	£3,250	£2,841	£2,932	£2,818	£2,730	£2,426	£2,375	£2,468	£2,308	£2,672	£2,689	£2,031	£2,790	£1,817
Total receipts	£4,381	£4,000	£3,800	£3,230	£3,031	£2,508	£2,485	£2,258	£2,200	£2,748	£2,799	£1,909	£2,360	£1,648
Net receipts	£1,131	£1,159	£868	£412	£301	£82	£110	-£210	-£108	£76	£110	-£122	-£430	-£169
Ratio expenditure/receipts	74%	71%	77%	87%	90%	97%	96%	109%	104%	97%	96%	106%		110%
Road vehicles														
Gross receipts												£1,159		
Expenditure												£856		
Net Receipts												£309		
Rolling stock														
Steam locomotives	3	3	3	3	3	3	3	3	3	3	3	3	3	3
Passenger carriages	8	8	8	8	8	8	8	7	8	7	7	8	8	8
Other coaching vehicles	1	1	1	1	1	1	1	1	1	1	1	1	1	1
Merchandise and mineral vehicles	18	18	18	18	18	18	19	19	19	26	26	26	27	27
Passenger road vehicles												9*	7	7

Goods and parcels road vehicles												
											2	
											2	* including four on hire
Posting	662	926	785	890	1,007	783	456	322	632	661		
	£47	£59	£50	£62	£55	£59	£37	£27	£43	£45		
Talyllyn coaches	9,226	7,522	8,652	8,278	8,918	6,033	4,929	4,205	3,351	5,117		
	£427	£344	£399	£380	£416	£275	£292	£260	£205	£473		
Coaching stock												
Composite 1st/3rd	3	3	3	3	3	3	4	4	4	5	5	5
3rd	5	5	5	5	5	5	4	3	4	2	3	3
Brake Van	1	1	1	1	1	1	1	1	1	1	1	1
Large iron wagons	6	6	6	6	6	6	6	6	6	6		
Small iron wagons	3	4	4	5	5	5	6	6	6	6		
Wooden wagons	7	6	6	5	5	5	5	5	10	10		
Timber trucks	2	2	2	2	2	2	2	2	4	4	2	
Directors' fees	50	50	50	50	50	0	0					
Salaries	250	250	250	250	250	230	250	250				

	1915	1916	1917	1918	1919	1920	1921	1922	1923	1924	1925	1926	1927	1928	1929	1930
Capital issued																
5% Debenture stock																
Total issued	£5,000	£5,000	£5,000	£5,000	£5,000	£5,000	£5,000	£5,000	£5,000	£5,000	£5,000	£5,000	£5,000	£5,000	£5,000	£5,000
Ordinary stock																
Total issued	£15,000	£15,000	£15,000	£15,000	£15,000	£15,000	£15,000	£15,000	£15,000	£15,000	£15,000	£15,000	£15,000	£15,000	£15,000	£15,000
Capital expenditure	£23,120					£23,245	£25,265							£25,924		
During year						£100								£389		
Revenue expenditure																
Maintenance of way and works	£318					£614		£604	£535	£535	£562	£572	£687	£686	£595	£218
Maintenance of carriages	£29					£23		£45	£98	£151	£60	£161	£72			
Maintenance of wagons	£50					£98		£41	£58	£78	£82	£20	£22			
Locomotive maintenance	£153					£238		£128	£204	£214	£365	£250	£348	£325	£567	£90
Loco running expenses	£296					£618		£702	£631	£587	£574	£533	£504	£440	£414	£188
Traffic expenses	£569					£1,392		£1,368	£1,226	£1,316	£1,302	£933	£1,112	£1,053	£1,096	£443
General charges	£279					£132		£558	£601	£530	£490	£664	£492	£545	£534	£246
Parliamentary and legal expenses										£2		£121	£36	£24		
Damage and loss of goods, property, &c								£11	£2	£5	£2		£3			
Rates	£71					£116		£46	£52	£42	£31	£35	£54	£46	£39	£10
Railway freight rebates fund - rate relief															£7	£11
Government duty	£14					£57		£4	£2	£2	£2	£2	£3	£2		
National insurance - health, pensions	£14					£20		£25	£24	£19	£21	£42	£42	£40	£38	£16
Ditto - unemployment	£1					£1		£10	£16	£11	£24	£14	£13	£9	£11	£5
Miscellaneous	£24							£22	£26	£27	£29	£30	£29	£29		
Total traffic expenditure	£1,818					£3,309		£3,564	£3,475	£3,519	£3,544	£3,377	£3,417	£3,199	£3,301	£1,227

Revenue receipts											
Passengers											
First class	£65	£94	£59	£54	£39	£48	£50	£56	£41	£31	£7
Third class	£609	£1,141	£1,258	£1,147	£1,195	£1,085	£1,133	£1,199	£1,099	£977	£350
Season tickets											
First class											
Third class	£8	£24	£49	£14	£6	£10	£5	£5	£8	£20	£12
Workmen's tickets	£8	£22	£23	£36	£36	£53	£59	£90	£73	£52	£21
Total receipts from passengers	£690	£1,281	£1,389	£1,251	£1,276	£1,196	£1,247	£1,350	£1,221	£1,080	£390
Parcels and other merchandise											
Parcels under 2cwt and excess luggage	£114	£180	£174	£162	£149	£153	£151	£217	£204	£208	£83
Other merchandise by passenger trains	£14	£8	£7	£8	£11	£7	£10	£28	£13	£13	£3
Mails and parcel post	£55	£55	£55	£55	£55	£55	£75	£104	£104	£104	£44
Total passenger train receipts	£873	£1,524	£1,625	£1,476	£1,491	£1,411	£1,483	£1,699	£1,542	£1,405	£520
Goods train traffic											
Merchandise	£270	£732	£220	£331	£467	£283	£209	£143	£133	£188	£63
Minerals	£408	£490	£369	£588	£619	£1,030	£1,152	£891	£826	£813	£363
Coal, coke and patent fuel	£81	£229	£260	£230	£196	£191	£144	£236	£236	£225	£89
Total goods train receipts	£759	£1,451	£849	£1,149	£1,282	£1,504	£1,505	£1,270	£1,195	£1,226	£515
Total traffic receipts	£1,818	£2,976	£2,474	£2,625	£2,773	£2,915	£2,988	£2,969	£2,737	£2,631	£1,035
Miscellaneous	£16	£2	£6	£15	£12	£12	£6	£6	£5	£7	£1
Total	£1,834	£2,978	£2,480	£2,640	£2,785	£2,927	£2,994	£2,975	£2,742	£2,638	£1,036
Revenue receipts and expenditure											
Gross receipts	£1,834	£2,978	£2,480	£2,640	£2,785	£2,927	£2,994	£2,975	£2,742	£2,638	£1,036
Expenditure	£1,818	£3,309	£3,564	£3,475	£3,519	£3,544	£3,377	£3,417	£3,199	£3,301	£1,227
Net receipts	£16	-£331	-£1,084	-£835	-£734	-£617	-£383	-£442	-£457	-£663	-£191
Passenger road vehicles											
Gross receipts	£285	£12	£626	£1,012	£4,212	£5,607	£5,882	£5,993	£6,220	£5,861	£1,815
Expenditure	£193	£84	£461	£821	£4,476	£5,552	£5,682	£5,594	£5,628	£5,803	£2,185

	1915	1916	1917	1918	1919	1920	1921	1922	1923	1924	1925	1926	1927	1928	1929	1930
Net receipts	£92					-£72		£165	£191	-£264	£53	£200	£399	£592	£48	£370
Total of the foregoing																
Gross receipts	£1,933							£3,106	£3,652	£6,997	£8,532	£8,876	£8,968	£9,291	£8,775	£2,975
Expenditure	£2,011							£4,025	£4,296	£7,995	£9,096	£9,059	£9,011	£9,128	£9,440	£3,557
Net receipts	-£78					-£404		-£919	-£644	-£998	-£564	-£183	-£43	£163	-£665	-£582
Net revenue and appropriation																
Net receipts	-£78						-£1,703	-£919	-£644	-£998	-£564	-£183	-£43	£163	-£665	-£582
Chief rents, wayleaves, etc														£29	£29	£11
Net revenue for the year														£134	-£694	-£593
Balance brought forward	-£2,110						-£4,208	-£5,911	-£6,830	-£7,478	-£8,476	-£9,040	-£9,223	-£9,266	-£9,132	-£9,826
Special items																£10,419
Balance carried forward	-£2,186					-£4,208	-£5,911	-£6,830	-£7,478	-£8,476	-£9,040	-£9,223	-£9,266	-£9,132	-£9,826	
Liabilities																
Capital account																
Amount due to bankers, temporary loans	£241				£361	£265	£591	£536	£67	£1,310	£1,328					
Accounts payable	£5,868				£7,852	£8,630	£11,811	£12,774	£13,939	£14,075	£15,148	£17,102	£16,942	£16,979	£17,767	
Liabilities accrued	£12				£12	£12	£12	£12	£12	£12	£12	£233	£237	£250	£280	
Balance available for dividends and general reserve	-£2,186				-£3,804	-£4,208	-£5,911	-£6,830	-£7,478	-£8,476	-£9,040	-£9,222	-£9,265	-£9,132	-£9,826	
Total	£3,935				£4,421	£4,699	£6,503	£6,492	£6,540	£6,921	£7,448	£8,113	£7,914	£8,097	£8,201	
Assets																
Capital account - balance	£3,120				£3,245	£3,345	£5,265	£5,265	£5,265	£5,486	£5,516	£5,516	£5,536	£5,924	£5,924	
Cash at bankers and in hand												£131	£167	£98	£183	
Investments																
Stock of stores and materials	£343				£419	£486	£429	£487	£387	£431	£698	£1,121	£1,178	£1,068	£1,076	
Outstanding traffic accounts	£36				£60	£119	£146	£95	£167	£162	£336	£421	£335	£329	£341	

	£436	£697	£749	£663	£645	£721	£842	£898	£924	£698	£678	£677	
Accounts receivable	£436	£697	£749	£663	£645	£721	£842	£898	£924	£698	£678	£677	
Balance sheet assets	£3,935	£4,421	£4,699	£6,503	£6,492	£6,540	£6,921	£7,448	£8,113	£7,914	£8,097	£8,201	
Maintenance - materials used													
Ballast (cu yd)	480				469	607	560	120	98	200	60	50	60
Fencing (ch)	340				60	34	38	51	30	32			
Rail (tons)	1												
Sleepers (No)	296				100	222	140	140	500	940	533	500	43
Rolling stock													
Steam locomotives	3	3	3	4	4	3	3	3	3	3	2	2	
Rolling stock													
Of uniform class	3	3	3	3	3	2	2	2	2	2	2	2	
Composite	5	5	5	5	5	5		5	5	5	5	5	
Luggage, parcel and brake vans	1	1	1	1	1	1	1	1	1	1	1	1	
Merchandise and mineral wagons													
Open wagons	21	16	16	17	16	16	16	16	16	16	12		
Rail and timber trucks	6	18	18	17	17	17	17	17	17	17	17		
Special wagons					1	1	1	1	1	1			
Brake vans							1	1	1	1			
Service rolling stock - other vehicles													
Construction and maintenance of rolling stock													
Charged to capital - locomotives													
Heavy repairs		1	1										
Light repairs	2	1	1	2	3	1	2	1	1	1	1	1	
Number under or awaiting repair at end of year	1	1	1	1	1	1	1	2	1	1	1	1	
Passenger carriages													
Light repairs	7	7	4	7	2	4	4	4	4	4	4	6	

	1915	1916	1917	1918	1919	1920	1921	1922	1923	1924	1925	1926	1927	1928	1929	1930
Number under or awaiting repair at end of year	1					1	1	1	1	1	1	1	1	2	2	
Other coaching vehicles																
Heavy repairs																
Merchandise and mineral vehicles																
Number of renewals	6				16	4						3	3			
Heavy repairs					6	4					3					
Light repairs	21				12	21		4	8	8	11	10	10	10	14	
Number under or awaiting repair at end of year						2										
Mileage run by engines																
Coaching	8,770				6,741	7,059	7,528	8,250	9,279	9,336	6,371	8,517	9,979	10,050	10,283	4,230
Freight	8,770				6,740	7,060	7,529	8,249	9,279	9,336	6,371	8,517	9,980	10,051	10,282	4,231
Shunting																
Steam locomotives	1,558				1,160	1,136	1,218	1,318	1,446	1,727	1,147	1,975	1,824	1,831	1,869	768
Other miles, assisting, light, etc																
Steam locomotives	808				509	515	364	439	178	54	7	261	169	49	23	24
Total engine miles	19,906				15,150	15,771	16,639	18,256	20,182	20,453	13,896	19,270	21,952	21,981	22,457	9,253
Passenger traffic																
First class	2,597				1,967	2,541	1,884	1,624	1,482	1,074	1,341	1,920	1,580	1,204	856	213
Third class	35,722				38,864	45,175	42,564	45,186	47,318	49,250	45,641	46,881	52,787	49,707	44,735	16,271
Total	38,319				40,831	47,716	44,448	46,180	48,800	50,324	46,982	48,801	54,367	50,911	45,591	16,484
Workmen (calculated on a single journey basis)	1,008				1,344	4,608	3,224	4,284	8,878	8,105	7,084	8,274	12,206	8,995	6,864	3,018
Total exclusive of season ticket holders	39,327				42,175	52,324	47,672	51,094	57,678	58,429	54,066	57,075	66,573	59,906	52,455	19,502
Season tickets																
Third class	8				45	21	37	70	21	3	5	2	3	4	83	39
Goods, mineral and livestock traffic																

Merchandise	2,125	5,052	5,878	1,721	1,842	2,091	3,639	1,484	801	613	521	1,003	414
Minerals	4,668	2,823	5,078	4,495	3,948	5,552	5,759	6,406	5,487	4,380	4,065	3,808	1,714
Coal	704	990	1,362	939	1,095	1,285	777	753	517	860	889	851	341
Total	7,497	8,865	12,318	7,155	6,885	8,928	10,175	8,643	6,805	5,853	5,475	5,662	2,469
Miscellaneous property													
Houses	3	3	3	3	3	3	3	3	3	3	3		
Road vehicles													
Motors (hired)	2	1	3	3	3	3	11	11	10	10	10		
Horse drawn	5	5	5	7	5	5	5	5	5	5	5		
Horse wagon and carts	2	2	2	2	2	2	2	2	2	2	2		
Horses (shunting)	3	4	4	3	1	3	3	2	2	2	2		
Horses (for road vehicles)	2	1	1	4	4	2	2	2	2	2	2		
Road transport											£591		
Gross receipts											£6,219		
Expenditure											£5,628		

Alfred James Lambert was the railway's chairman from 1879 until his death on 22 September 1891. He is buried close to the architect Nicholas Hawksmoor and the racing driver Graham Hill in the churchyard of St Botolph's, Shenleybury, Herts.

PAYMENTS TO IMPERIAL TRAMWAYS

Extracted from the Corris Railway Company's annual reports

	£	£
June 1885	150	
	100	
July 1885	100	350
January 1886	150	
February 1886	100	
July 1886	150	400
March 1887	200	
April 1887	100	
September 1887	200	
December 1887	100	600
April 1888	100	
August 1888	200	300
February 1889	150	
July 1889	100	250
February 1890	300	
September 1890	100	400
July 1891	200	
December 1891	100	300
January 1892	100	
February 1892	100	
April 1892	50	
May 1892	100	350
	2950	2950

MILEAGE 1900-13

Extracted from the Corris Railway Company's annual reports

	1900	1901	1902	1903	1904	1905	1906	1907	1908	1909	1910	1911	1912	1913
Passenger	14570	14476	14565	14488	15471	14840	13990	16199	25718	25001	23385	23305		
Goods	10083	10444	10564	10333	9894	7819	7100	7300	3222	3402	3369	3606		
Mixed														20751
	24653	24920	25129	24821	25365	22659	21090	23499	28940	28403	26754	26911		20751
Shunting														1540
Assisting, light														794
														23085

The village terminus of the Upper Corris Tramway ended where this footpath joins Bryn Idris in the centre of this photograph.

PLANNING APPLICATIONS 2001-11

Gwynedd Council

Application		Decision	
23 January 2001	Full application for proposed platform and yard extension	Approved	20 March 2001
23 January 2001	Full application for proposed toilets and septic tank	Approved	20 March 2001
23 January 2001	Application for listed building consent for proposed toilets and septic tank	Approved	23 April 2001
23 January 2001	Full application for renewal of engine shed doors, replacement of windows and construction of retaining wall	Approved	20 March 2001
23 January 2001	Application for listed building consent for renewal of engine shed doors, replacement of windows and construction of retaining wall	Approved	23 April 2001
23 January 2001	Retrospective application for a signal cabin	Approved	20 March 2001
19 December 2003	Full application to construct embankment and retaining gabion for deviation of course of narrow gauge railway together with accommodation works	Approved	8 March 2010
11 May 2004	Construction of shed for storage of train carriages	Approved	20 July 2004
31 August 2011	Redevelopment scheme to include demolition of station buildings, toilet block and Portakabin to allow erection of railway terminus and toilet building, realign railway track, erection Health Centre with bus shelter and alterations to boundary wall.	Approved	18 October 2011

Snowdonia National Park Authority

22 January 2004	Maespoeth, Pont y Goedwig, Corris. Construction of embankment and retaining gabion, construction of deviation of course of narrow gauge railway together with accommodation works.	Approved	6 April 2011

BIBLIOGRAPHY

Booth, T.; The Corris Railway; *Railway Magazine*, June 1898

Boyd, J.I.C.; *Narrow Gauge Railways in Mid-Wales*; Oakwood Press, 2nd edition, 1970

Briwnant-Jones, G.; *Great Western Corris*; Gomer Press, 1994

Briwnant-Jones, G.; *The Last Days of the Old Corris*; Gomer Press, 2001

Coleman, D.K.; J.R. Dix; *Journal of the Corris Railway Society*, 1985, 1986

Corris Railway Company Ltd; *Dossier containing details of the Company's plans for re-opening the section of the Corris Railway from Corris to Tan y Coed*; Corris Railway Company, 5th edition January 1993

Cozens, Lewis; *The Corris Railway*; Author, 1949, reissued with notes by the Corris Railway Society 1972, 1977, 1987 and 1992

Fuller, Martin; *Talyllyn & Corris Steam Locomotives Volume 1 Pre-preservation and manufacturers*; Author, 2014

Fuller, Martin; *Talyllyn & Corris Steam Locomotives Volume 2 Early preservation and locomotive rebuilds*; Author, 2017

Fuller, Martin; *Talyllyn & Corris Steam Locomotives – the appendices*; Author, 2018

Gasquoine, G.P.; *The Story of the Cambrian – a biography of a railway*; Woodall, Minshall, Thomas & Co, 1922

Green, C.C.; *The Coast Lines of the Cambrian Railways Volume 1 Machynlleth to Aberystwyth*; Wild Swan 1993

Greenhough, Richard; Sir Clifton Robinson; *Journal of the Corris Railway Society*, 1990

Greenhough, Richard; The Corris Carriages; *Journal of the Corris Railway Society*, 1979

Greenhough, Richard; The Corris Railway Traffic in the 1920s and 1930s; *Journal of the Corris Railway Society*, 1988

Greenhough, Richard; Corris Conservation; *Railway Magazine*, March 1988

Jenkins, Stanley, C.; The Cork, Blackrock and Passage Railway; Oakwood Press, 2nd enlarged edition, 1993

Johnson, Peter; *The Cambrian Railways - a new history*; Oxford Publishing Co, 2013

Jones, Gwyn Briwnant; *Tales of the Old Corris*; Gomer Press, 2008

Morgan, John Scott; *Corris – a narrow gauge portrait*; Irwell Press, 1991

Rees, James; Our Newest Recruit – the Corris Railway; *Great Western Railway Magazine*, September 1930

Richards, Alun John; *Slate Quarrying at Corris*; Carreg Gwalch, 1994

Vignes, Edouard (Translated by D.A. Boreham); *A Technical Study of the Festiniog & other narrow gauge railways*; P. E. Waters & Associates, 1986

INDEX

Machynlleth viewed from Foel y Fridd before 1930, the GWR station slightly to the left of centre. The pedestrian ramp provided for passengers moving between the stations can be seen climbing up the embankment. A motor bus is parked outside the Corris station.

In September 1940 No 3 was caught threading its way through Corris with a rake of slab wagons bound for Aberllefenni.

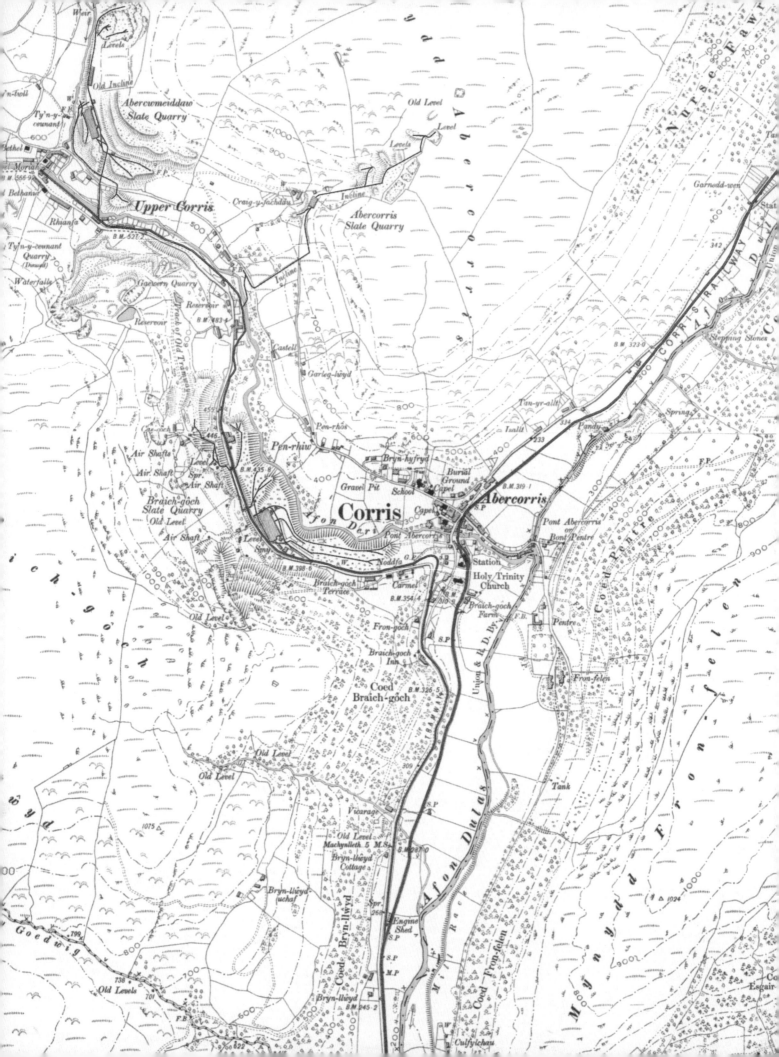